LANGSTON HUGHES

in the Hispanic World and Haiti

edited by EDWARD J. MULLEN

Archon Books
1977

Library of Congress Cataloging in Publication Data

Hughes, Langston, 1902-1967.
 Langston Hughes in the Hispanic world and Haiti.

 "Langston Hughes's works translated into Spanish": p.
 Bibliography: p.
 Includes index.
 CONTENTS: The literary reputation of Langston Hughes
in the Hispanic world and Haiti.—Prose: Mexico: Mexican
games. In a Mexican city. The Virgin of Guadalupe. Up to the
crater of an old volcano. Love in Mexico. Cuba: A Cuban
sculptor. Haiti: White shadows in a Black land. An appeal for
Jacques Roumain. Spain: Too much of race. Negroes in Spain.
Laughter in Madrid. Essays from the Afro-American.—Poetry:
Air raid, Barcelona. From Spain to Alabama. Hero, Interna-
tional Brigade. Letter from Spain addressed to Alabama. [etc.]
 1. Civilization, Hispanic—Literary collections. 2. Hughes,
Langston, 1902-1967—Criticism and interpretation—Ad-
dresses, essays, lectures. I. Mullen, Edward J., 1942- II. Title.
PS3515.U274A6 1977   818'.5'209   77-3388
ISBN 0-208-01634-1

©Edward J. Mullen 1977

The poem "to Arthur Spingarn" (page 159)
© George Houston Bass, Trustee of the
Estate of Langston Hughes 1977

First published 1977 as an Archon Book,
an imprint of The Shoe String Press, Inc.
Hamden, Connecticut 06514

Printed in the United States of America

To the memory of Langston Hughes (1902–1967), who wanted America to be America again.

Contents

III. ¿Quién es Langston Hughes?

Preface

Langston Hughes (1902-1967), born in Joplin, Missouri, is among the world's most famous black writers. In 1942 he succinctly described his intellectual formation and broad travels in the following way:

My chief literary influences have been Paul Laurence Dunbar, Carl Sandburg, and Walt Whitman. My favorite public figures include Jimmy Durante, Marlene Dietrich, Mary McLeod Bethune, Mrs. Franklin D. Roosevelt, Marian Anderson, and Henry Armstrong. I live in Harlem, New York City. I am unmarried. I like: *Tristan,* goat's milk, short novels, lyric poems, heat, simple folk, boats, and bullfights; I dislike *Aida,* parsnips, long novels, narrative poems, cold, pretentious folk, busses, and bridge. . . .

My writing has been largely concerned with the depicting of Negro life in America. I have made a number of translations of the poems of Negro writers in Cuba and Haiti. In 1931-32 I lectured throughout the South in the Negro schools and colleges there, and one of my main interests is the encouragement of literary ability among colored writers. The winter of 1934 I spent in Mexico, where I translated a number of Mexican and Cuban stories. I was the only American Negro newspaper correspondent in Spain, in 1937—for the Baltimore *Afro-American.* I am executive director of the Harlem Suitcase Theatre, the only Negro Workers' Theatre in New York. I received the *Palms* Intercollegiate Poetry Award in 1927, the Harmon Award of Literature in 1931, in 1934 was selected by Dr. Charles A. Beard as one of America's twenty-five "most interesting" personages

with a "socially conscious" attitude, and in 1935 was granted a
Guggenheim Fellowship for creative work.[1]

Rightfully called the "dean of black letters," Hughes was the member
of the Harlem Renaissance movement whose influence was the most
pervasive and sustained in American literature. As the foremost
chronicler of the black experience in America, Mr. Hughes's output
was prodigious: poems, plays, essays, short stories, opera librettos,
and newspaper columns. Roy Wilkins, in a eulogy published after
Hughes's death in May 1967, described the magnitude of his impact
on the lives of black Americans:

> We do not know quite what to say about Langston's passing
> from us except that it deprives members of his race and his
> fellow Americans of something precious that eased many a
> weary period of their lives. We count it a special privilege that it
> was the official magazine of the National Association for the
> Advancement of Colored People, *The Crisis,* which gave
> Langston his first publication anywhere in 1921 when it
> appeared with his poem "The Negro Speaks of Rivers." He went
> on to a worldwide fame rooted firmly in the affection his people
> had for him and in his understanding of and devotion to their
> trials and tribulations, his heralding of their triumphs and his
> spreading of their folk philosophy.
>   Of many men it is said "We shall not see his like again," but
> this tribute applies in truth to Langston who won our love in his
> own special way. He gave to people his riches of cheer, of
> compassion, of righteous indignation over wrongs. We are sure
> he would not have us grieve, but smile a wry and knowing smile,
> remark on an imperfect world, laugh a deep laugh, sing a heart
> song and keep climbing life's hard paths which, as he truly
> wrote, "ain't been no crystal stair" for his wonderful people.[2]

Although considerable attention has been focused in recent years
on the role Hughes played in twentieth-century American literature,
virtually no interest has been directed toward his influence in the
broader sphere of international black literature.[3] The purpose of this
book is to bring his writings on the Hispanic world and Haiti
together with an essay tracing his influence and literary contacts in

the Spanish-speaking world and the Caribbean. These materials range from his first essay published in an American magazine to his description of Spain during the Civil War. Collectively these texts form an important chronicle of the black experience on an international level and add one more link in the chain of evidence for his stature as a writer of world-wide importance.

I would like to express my appreciation to the following for their assistance: Professor Paul Rogers for his careful reading of the manuscript; Professor Harold Jones for securing rare materials from the Biblioteca del Ayuntamiento in Madrid; Professor David Arthur McMurray for supplying considerable information on Nicolás Guillén, and the various librarians at Fisk University, Howard University, New York Public Library, the University of Missouri-Columbia, and Yale University for their help in locating materials.

I gratefully acknowledge the support the University of Missouri-Columbia Research Council gave this investigation.

---

[1] *Twentieth Century Authors*, ed. Stanley J. Kunitz and Howard Haycraft (New York: H. W. Wilson, 1942), p. 684. Of considerable interest as well are the lively comments of Carl Van Vechten in "Introducing Langston Hughes to the Reader," *The Weary Blues* (New York: Alfred Knof, 1926), pp. 9–13.

[2] "Langston Hughes: A Tribute," *The Crisis* 74 (June 1967): 246.

[3] An interesting exception is the essay of Thomas A. Hale, "From Afro-America to Afro-France: The Literary Triangle Trade," *French Review* 49 (May 1976): 1089–96.

Acknowledgments

The author wishes to thank the publishers and holders of copyright for their permission to reprint the following material:

"The Virgin of Guadalupe," from *The Crisis*, December 1921, p. 77. Reprinted by permission of *The Crisis*.

"Love in Mexico," from *Opportunity*, April 1940, pp. 107–108. Reprinted with permission of the National Urban League.

"A Cuban Sculptor," from *Opportunity*, November 1930, p. 334. Reprinted with permission of the National Urban League.

"White Shadows in a Black Land," from *The Crisis*, May 1932, p. 157. Reprinted by permission of *The Crisis*.

"An Appeal for Jacques Romain," reprinted by permission of *The New Republic*. Copyright 1934 by the New Republic, Inc.

"Too Much of Race," from *The Volunteer for Liberty*, August 1937. Reprinted by permission of The Veterans of the Abraham Lincoln Brigade.

"Negroes in Spain," from *The Volunteer for Liberty*, September 1937. Reprinted by permission of the Veterans of the Abraham Lincoln Brigade.

"Laughter in Madrid," from *The Nation*, January 1938, pp. 123–24. Reprinted by permission of The Nation Company, Inc.

Articles appearing in the *Baltimore Afro-American* on 23 October 1937, p. 1 and p. 2, col. 6; 30 October 1937, p. 1 and p. 2, col. 1–3; 6 November 1937, p. 1; 20 November 1937, p. 3; 27 November 1937, p. 3; 11 December 1937, p. 3; 18 December 1937, p. 13; 1 January 1938, p. 2; 8 January 1938, p. 2; 15 January 1938, p. 17; 22 January 1938, p. 2; 5 February 1938, p. 5; 12 February 1938, p. 6 and an anonymous article "Afro Writer Nicked by Bullet," 29 January 1938, p. 5. Reprinted courtesy Afro-American Newspapers.

"Air Raid Barcelona," from *Esquire*, October 1938, p. 40. Reprinted by permission of *Esquire Magazine*, copyright 1938 by Esquire, Inc.

"From Spain to Alabama," from *Experiment*, 1949, p. 276. Reprinted by permission of *Experiment*, copyright 1949 by *Experiment*.

"Hero International Brigade," from *The Heart of Spain*, Veterans of the Abraham Lincoln Brigade, 1952, pp. 325–26. Reprinted by permission of the Veterans of the Abraham Lincoln Brigade.

"Letter from Spain Addressed to Alabama," from *The Volunteer for Liberty,* November 1937. Reprinted by permission of the Veterans of the Abraham Lincoln Brigade.

"Moonlight in Valencia," reprinted by permission of Harold Ober Associates, Inc.

"Put Out the Lights and Stop the Clocks," reprinted by permission of Harold Ober Associates, Inc. Copyright 1977 by George Houston Bass.

"Song of Spain," reprinted by permission of Harold Ober Associates, Inc. Copyright 1938 by Langston Hughes. Copyright renewed 1965 by Langston Hughes.

The Literary Reputation of Langston Hughes in the Hispanic World and Haiti

A few months after the death of Langston Hughes, Conrad Kent Rivers wrote the following lines in tribute to the poet:

> Some people I am acquainted with thought that Langston Hughes had passed through our world long before his actual death. Too often I have heard black artists read his last will. I am of the opinion that Langston Hughes and his body of work constitute the essence of Negritude. We cannot afford the luxury of a white Eliot or a Spanish Lorca without the necessity of a black Hughes. Langston was all I had as a youth to hang on to. We understood his poetry, and certainly it was not all a galaxy of masterpieces, but it was the real thing.[1]

Rivers's comments call attention to the somewhat ambivalent status Hughes held in the realm of American letters. Although at the time of his death Hughes was generally recognized as among the most important black North American writers of the twentieth century and was on the verge of entering the mainstream of contemporary American letters,[2] it is ironic that at that time he was more widely known in the Hispanic world than in the country of his birth. His case calls to mind that of Edgar Allan Poe and Walt Whitman, who for a time were far better received in France and Spanish America than in the United States. The reason for Hughes's prominence in the Hispanic world and the influence of Hispanic motifs in his own work arise from a complex set of factors, both historical and aesthetic,

---

Notes to this chapter are on page 39.

which offer new evidence of the truly international role Hughes played in world literature. It is the purpose of this essay to trace Hughes's involvement in the Hispanic world.[3]

Hughes's relationship to the Spanish-speaking world was of considerable importance to him, both personally and in the development of his work. His role as a cultural mediator was first pointed out in 1937 by Nancy Cunard:

> He has battled from the start for the liberation of the Scottsboro martyrs, and has been a link between Latin-American and American culture, besides being an excellent translator, and one ever ready to help young poets. Yes, Langston Hughes is the traveling star of coloured America, the leader of the young intellectuals.[4]

In a letter to Blanche Knopf dated 5 August 1940, he wrote concerning the translation of his autobiography into Spanish:

> So far I think I have forgotten to mention to you the fact that there might be some sales and translation possibilities for *The Big Sea* in Latin America. Many of my poems and several of my short stories have appeared in translation in various countries down there, and I am in two Latin American anthologies of Negro verse in Spanish.[5]

It is not surprising that Hughes felt strongly about the 1968 publication of *Yo también soy América* (*I, Too, am America*),[6] an anthology of his selected poems in Spanish with a preface by Andrés Henestrosa. As Ernesto Mejía Sánchez said: Hughes "considered that undertaking to be the high point of his career, on a par with the publication of his *Selected Poems*."[7]

I. Mexico

Hughes's relationship with the Spanish-speaking world was focussed at three seminal moments in his life: his travels to Mexico, the Caribbean, and Spain.[8] Hughes's association with Mexico was long, fruitful, and in many ways the most meaningful to him as a writer. He first traveled to Mexico when he was about five or six years old with his mother, who was attempting a reconciliation with Langston's father, the manager of an electric plant in Toluca.[9] Langston's mother could not tolerate life in Mexico and they went back to the United States almost immediately. Langston returned again to spend a summer with his father in the spring of 1919. That summer, according to the poet "the most miserable I have ever known,"[10] was spent in brooding isolation in Toluca. Lured by the prospect of money for college, Hughes returned to see his father once again in the summer of 1920 and remained until September 1921. It was en route to Mexico City that he composed his most often anthologized poem, "A Negro Speaks of Rivers."[11]

Mary White Ovington described Hughes's early Mexican experience in these words:

> Langston Hughes found himself far up in the mountains, at Yoluca, [sic] the highest habitable valley in Mexico. The place was beautiful, but very cold. And the father was cold, a business man, who measured life in terms of money and profit. He was assistant manager in an electric light plant, and was also in charge of a number of estates, abandoned by their owners in the revolution. He himself had lost a good deal because of the unstable government. A prodigious worker, he could keep at his tasks eighteen hours a day without diversion. He wanted his son to be interested in the business, offering to educate him if he would go abroad away from race prejudice! While in Yoluca, Langston taught English in a Mexican school, and to his disgust grew pedantic in his own speech. Despite the romantic surroundings, the life in Mexico was hard, drab. Two temperaments were clashing; two Negroes were showing opposing attitudes on the color problem. The father wished his handsome, clever son to abandon America and his race. He should study abroad and then return to Mexico, where the two would grow prosperous together. The son wanted something quite different. If he went to college, it should be in America. If he worked, it should not be at the blinding pace that left no energy for the gay, youthful things of life. Moreover, he had no desire to separate himself from the race to which his mother belonged. He was devoted to his mother—worker in white women's

kitchens but valiant fighter against race prejudice. His father was alien to him. So after a year they compromised, the son returning to the United States to study at Columbia and receiving some financial help.[12]

Although his personal relationship with his father remained poor, from a literary standpoint it was an extremely productive period in his life. He began to learn Spanish well by reading the novels of Vicente Blasco Ibañez, *Caños y barro* and *Cuentos valencianos,* and wrote some of his first published poems and essays. The only poem with a specifically Mexican setting, "Mexican Market Woman," appeared in *Crisis* in 1922.[13] Hughes later spoke of the poem's genesis in a recording:

> In Mexico once I wrote a poem about . . . an Indian peasant woman from the hills. I lived in Toluca where there was a big market. And this old woman had come into town one day with a bag of vegetables on her back that she spread out on the earth in the market place to sell. So I wrote:

> > This ancient hag
> > Who sits upon the ground
> > Selling her scanty wares
> > Day in, day round,
> > Has known high wind-swept mountains,
> > And the sun has made
> > Her skin so brown.[14]

Hughes also published three short prose sketches in a journal recently founded by Dr. W. E. DuBois, *The Brownies Book.*[15] "Mexican Games," his first essay published in an American magazine, appeared in January 1921.[16] It was followed in April by "In a Mexican City,"[17] a description of market-day Toluca, and in December by "Up to the Crater of an Old Volcano,"[18] an account of a trip to Xinantécatl near Toluca. The same month *Crisis* published a very brief note, "The Virgin of Guadalupe."[19]

From a literary point of view these short pieces are not particularly impressive. It must be remembered, however, that they were written for children and that Hughes was only nineteen at the time of their composition. Drewey W. Gunn put it best when he wrote:

> In December 1921 *Crisis* had also published his prose version of
> the legend of the Virgin of Guadalupe. . . . "Mexican Games,"
> . . . simply gives three games that he had seen the children in
> Toluca playing. Later in the year "In a Mexican City" and "Up
> to the Crater of an Old Volcano" appeared. Since both are in a
> language appropriate to children, they do not give us much
> indication of Hughes' great skill with the rhythms of American
> speech. In the one he takes a tourist's view of Toluca, speaking
> particularly of the fiestas, the homes, and the markets; in the
> other he tells about a walking tour he made with students from
> the Instituto to the nearby Nevado de Toluca. *The Big Sea*
> provides a more interesting view of life in the provincial town.[20]

During his weekend trips to Mexico City, Hughes met the young
poet Carlos Pellicer[21] who was a member of an important literary
circle known as the *Contemporáneos* ("Contemporaries"). In an
interview on 5 June 1972, Pellicer recalled his friendship with
Hughes. "I knew Langston well. He lived in Toluca for a year and
later on he spent some time in Mexico City. He spoke Spanish well.
In North American literature he is a noble, forgotten poet." It was
through Pellicer that Hughes was introduced to the playright and
poet Xavier Villaurrutia (1902–1950) and the essayist Salvador Novo
(1904–1973). It was Villaurrutia who published translations of four of
Hughes's early poems in *Contemporáneos*[22] in the fall of 1931. Novo
also identified Hughes in an important essay on black poetry
published in the same issue. Novo's essay, one of the first assessments
of the black literary renaissance of the twenties in Spanish America,
is also among the earliest comments on the innate racism of North
American literature. The text, in part, reads:

> Meanwhile, his muscular, sensual music, powerful as a
> primitive cry, has taken the United States by storm. The
> "Blues," which are as popular with a pullman porter as with the
> millionaire passenger, and the *Lap* have variously succeeded in
> uniting white man and black man, who both express through
> dance the joy of reproducing the ancestral impulses we all carry
> in our Jungian collective consciousness. For black poets of the

United States, the blues have opened another doorway to success. They cultivate the "blues" with a preferential delight. And then there is a Sherwood Anderson, who offers them a model of refined primitivism, and a Vachel Lindsay, who has sung his earthy rhythms, while for women there is a Sara Teasdale to imitate. Little by little, black poets—like the Jews, like the Italians—are going to abandon dialect. The universal recognition of their quality as poets (their poetry is beginning to appear in European reviews and anthologies) will inspire them to continue a work which already displays characteristics of singular value, but whose aspiration still appears to be a desire to fuse with the whole of American poetry, whose colors blur the governing characteristics of black poetry.

The first black known to have written poetry in the United States is Phyllis Wheatly. The first to be brought into the mainstream of American poetry is Paul Laurence Dunbar. From this great poet forward there are no less than twenty black poets of considerable quality, such as Richard Bruce, Waring Cunney, and Edward S. Silvera, all born in 1906. Countee Cullen, author of three books of verse and an anthology of black poetry and Langston Hughes, of whom translations have appeared in *Sur* recently, were born in 1903 and 1904 respectively. Langston Hughes is certainly one of the most interesting black poets today. A vagabond, he spent fifteen months in Mexico where he learned Spanish, taught English, went to the bullfights, and wrote his first published poem, "A Negro Speaks of Rivers." From Mexico he went to New York and then on to Africa and Europe, working on a steamship. He has been a waiter in a caberet in Montmartre and a cook in a black nightclub. He was discovered by Vachel Lindsay.[23]

The importance of Hughes's association with the journal *Contemporáneos*[24] cannot be overstated since it was widely recognized in the Hispanic world as one of the most important vanguard reviews.[25] In March 1931, Rafael Lozano published translations of seven poems and a short essay "Langston Hughes: El poeta afroestadounidense" ("Langston Hughes: Afro-American poet) in *Crisol,* a short-lived magazine of proletarian art. Lozano's comments, which are among the earliest critical assessments of Hughes's verse in Spanish, stress the then popular theory that black writers possessed a natural "primitive" spontaneity:

> Langston Hughes's poetry is highly spontaneous. It has that natural negligence born of emotion of which Charles Guerin speaks. He [Hughes] sings the same to Harlem prostitutes as to Mexican market women. But in all of his lines, the personal note is evident. His observation is direct and vital, intensely lived and felt with a violence approaching paroxysm. His poetry is neither overly realistic nor is it like that of Mallarmé; it has not even suffered the influence of the Baudelaire of *L'Albatros* ("The Albatross") or of the love for the exotic. It is a primitive composition, like all of the poetry of his race, which expresses itself, like jazz music, with its own slightly syncopated rhythm.[26]

In the fall of 1934 Hughes learned of the death of his father and returned to Mexico to settle the estate.[27] He remained until the spring of 1935, living as close as he had ever come to *la vie de bohème* in the company of writers and artists such as Juan de la Cabada, María Izquierdo, Luis Cardoza y Aragón, Manuel Bravo, Rufino Tamayo, and Nellie Campobello. He later recalled the impact of the experience on his life as a writer:

> For me it was a delightful winter. I have an affinity for Latin Americans, and the Spanish language I have always loved. One of the first things I did when I got to Mexico City was to get a tutor, a young woman friend of the Patiños, and began to read *Don Quixote* in the original, a great reading experience that possibly helped me to develop many years later in my own books a character called Simple. I also began to translate into English a number of Mexican short stories and poems by young writers for publication in the United States. I met a number of painters, the sad Orozco, the talkative Siqueiros, and the genteel Montenegro, whose studio was across the street from where I lived.[28]

For a while he shared an apartment with the French photographer Henry Cartier-Bresson and the Mexican folklorist Andrés Henestrosa.[29] In the spring of 1931 his friend, the Cuban diplomat

José Antonio Fernández de Castro, published an essay in the important daily *El Nacional,* "Langston Hughes, poeta militante negro" ("Langston Hughes, Militant Black Poet"). This article, which reintroduced Hughes to the Mexican public, contains a brief biography of the poet along with a number of observations on his poetry. Continuing the perspective voiced by Rafael Lozano, Fernández de Castro presents Hughes primarily as a poet *engagé* and spokesman for the black proletariat. This essay, which reflects a romanticized vision of blacks popular in the thirties, displays Hughes as a quintessential black poet: jovial, spontaneous, and possessed of an innate sense of natural "rhythm."

> The poetry of Langston Hughes is artistic because it is so deeply popular. By expressing the sorrows of his black brothers, he fulfills his duty as an artist. Up where one finds a "black sadness" produced by a white injustice, there, too, we find Langston Hughes who will gather this gloom in his poetry and sing it to the world. . . . But since the very nature of the black man is strength, a strength so worthy of imitation, . . . the black man doesn't just complain. He knows how to laugh at sorrow. And since Langston Hughes is black . . . he laughs as well. His poems are filled with laughter, color, sound, and splendor—the qualities of the black soul.[30]

It was followed in a matter of days by an article by the Guatemalan Luis Cardoza y Aragón in the same newspaper, "Langston Hughes el poeta de los negros" ("Langston Hughes, Poet of the Blacks").[31] Hughes's rapport with the *Contemporáneos* continued to be strong and in 1938 Xavier Villaurrutia dedicated a poem entitled "North Carolina Blues," which contained a reference to Jim Crowism, to his American friend.

> In different waiting rooms
> awaiting the same death
> the passengers of color
> and the whites, first-class.
>
> [En diversas salas de espera
> aguardan la misma muerte

> los pasajeros de color
> y los blancos, de primera.][32]

Hughes's association with various literary groups in the thirties, from the apolitical *Contemporáneos* to the left wing LEAR (League of Revolutionary Artists and Writers), led to a general popularity in artistic circles. For example, in 1938 the important Mexican novelist Mauricio Magdaleno published translations of "Cross" and "I, Too, Sing America" in *La Nueva Democracia* (August 1938, p. 15); and the following year the Mexican composer, Silvestre Revueltas set some of his poems to music.[33] Hughes's most important translator in Mexico, Manuel González Flores, who says he first read Hughes's poetry in the literary supplement of a Sunday paper,[34] began in 1945 to publish translations of some of his best-known poems.[35] Humberto Tejera reminisced about a chance meeting with the poet on 14 April 1935 in a brief note, "Langston Hughes en México" published in *El Nacional* (28 November 1948, pp. 5 and 28). In 1952, two short essays appeared in *El Nacional* in the literary column "El Ruiseñor y la prosa" ("The Nightingale and Writing") by Raúl Ortiz Avila. On 20 April 1952 the critic commented on González Flores's translation of *Freedom Train* and in his second essay (27 April 1952) discussed Hughes's early days in Toluca. In 1961 the prestigious literary review *Nivel* brought together a number of earlier translations with a dedicatory note, "El gran poeta norteamericano Langston Hughes" ("The Great American Poet Langston Hughes").[36] This same feature also contains a short critical note by the French scholar, Jean Wagner.

As recently as February 1976, the editor of *Nivel,* Germán Pardo García, wrote a brief note of eulogy:

> A dignified follower of the tradition of Martin Luther King, of Robenson . . . Langston Hughes is one of the most noble precursors of the emancipation from slavery, an institution still alive in America and other parts of the world. . . .
> Langston Hughes from the beginning sent out a cry of alarm which continues to echo in the heart of suffering people, who search for their ultimate redemption: "I am, too, America."[37]

During the sixties Hughes became the idol of a new generation of socially committed poets. Abigael Bohórquez published a rambling attack on capitalism in his "Carta abierta a Langston Hughes" ("Open Letter to Langston Hughes"),[38] an imitation of Hughes's "Open Letter to the South," and Hughes was eulogized posthumously by Leopoldo Ayala in "Réquiem para la tumba de un cuerpo" ("Requiem for the Tomb of a Body").[39]

In Bohórquez's piece, a violent and angry diatribe against racism, Langston Hughes emerges as a black Christ figure:

> Oh, Langston Hughes,
> because they can no longer restrain their petulance nor their
>   schizophrenia,
> because they can no longer find anything to do with the
>   Rockefeller Center building,
> with UNESCO,
> and their magnate hill "Four Presidents" of Dakota,
> because they don't know what to do with themselves,
> and their Navy,
> and their hot dogs,
> Black Jesus
> now I want you:
> Embrace me if you wish,
> embrace me.

> [Ay, Langston Hughes,
> porque ya no les cabe la petulancia ni la esquizofrenia,
> porque ya no hallan qué hacer con su edificio del Rockefeller
>   Center,
> de la Unesco,
> y su cerro magnate "Cuatro Presidentes" de Dakota,
> porque ya no hallan qué hacer con ellos mismos,
> y su Marina,
> y sus Hot Dogs,
> Negro-Jesucristo,
> ahora te quiero:
> Si quieres abrazarme,
> abrázame.]

It is ironic that Hughes's earliest literary contacts in Mexico (above all Novo and Villaurrutia) had been clearly apolitical, for he was eventually to become inextricably identified with the Left. The comments of the Mexican critic, Antonio Acevedo Escobedo, point to this problem. He writes that he met Hughes around 1936 at a meeting of the League of Revolutionary Artists and Writers, "a Leftist group of the Cárdenas period, which tried to emphasize this aspect of Langston's work, in spite of the fact that his poetry is universalist."[40] It appears that Hughes last visited Mexico in 1962.[41]

Apparently Hughes's early relationship to the Hispanic world was due to many factors, at least some of them were merely accidental: the trip to Mexico for reasons of financial expediency and his encounter with the *Contemporáneos* poets are cases in point. What initially may have been the result of chance was soon transformed by Hughes into one of the most powerful experiences of his life, for the language and people of Mexico seem to appeal to him somewhat as did the Harlem "language," scenes, and people.

II. Cuba

The Caribbean, and Cuba in particular, was an important point of contact between Hughes and the Spanish-speaking world. He first traveled to Cuba in the summer of 1927 while working as a mess boy on a freighter named the *Nardo*. The trip, a brief and unpleasant one, was recalled in his short story, "Powder-White Faces," which deals with racial discrimination in the brothels of Havana.[42] It is significant that Hughes published three poems with distinctly Hispanic landscapes in *The Weary Blues* ("Caribbean Sunset," "Soledad: A Cuban Portrait," and "To the Dark Mercedes of 'El Palacio de Amor'") one year prior to his actual trip to Havana.

In September 1928, the Cuban journalist José Antonio Fernández de Castro published the first Spanish translation of a poem by Hughes, "Yo también honro América" ("I, Too") in the Cuban journal *Social*. He first saw the poem in Countee Cullen's anthology *Caroling Dusk* (1927), sent to him by the American critic Lewis S. Gannet, and had read Hughes's biography in Mary White Ovington's *Portraits in Color*.[43] The text of this important translation reads:

Yo, También . . .

Yo, también, honro a América
Soy el hermano negro.
Me mandan a comer en la cocina,
Cuando vienen visitas . . .
Pero me río,
Como bien
Y así me fortalezco.

Mañana
Me sentaré en la mesa
Y aunque vengan visitas
Nadie se atreverá
A decirme
"A la cocina, negro."
Al mismo tiempo
Se darán cuenta
De lo hermoso que soy
Y se avergonzarán.
¡Yo soy también América![44]

Apart from his brief stop in Havana in 1927, Hughes made two important trips to Cuba. In February 1930 he spent two weeks in search of a black composer to collaborate with him on an opera commissioned by a patron in New York.[45] At this same period he met José Antonio Fernández de Castro by means of a letter of introduction given to him by Miguel Covarrubias whom he had met previously in Harlem and who had done illustrations for *The Weary Blues*.[46] In March 1930, Fernández de Castro published an introductory essay, "Presentación de Langston Hughes" in the *Revista de la Habana*. The Cuban's comments, essentially a paraphrase of Carl Van Vechten's preface to *The Weary Blues,* "Introducing Langston Hughes to the Reader," stress in particular Hughes's sense of racial pride:

> In the lyrical works of L. H.—as in those of Countee Cullen, Walter F. White, Jessie Faucet, Claude McKay, to name only the most representative black writers in the United States—a vigorous racial pride is evident, a combativeness unknown by the intellectual writers of that race until the present. His

technique is modern and with this sensitivity he achieves very personal touches which make him stand out as unique in the complicated panorama of contemporary poetic production in the United States. L.H., during his recent visit to Cuba, was received and entertained by representatives of our young intellectuals, and by distinguished and important black Cubans.[47]

As Fernández de Castro also states, it was he who introduced Hughes to poets such as José Zacarías Tallet, Regino Pedroso, Juan Marinello, and Nicolás Guillén. The last interviewed Hughes and published the text of his "Conversación con Langston Hughes" in the literary supplement, "Ideales de una Raza," of the newspaper *Diario de la Marina* on 9 March 1930.[48] This meeting led to a long and fruitful friendship which was later renewed in Spain during the Civil War. The interview is an important document, since it signals the deep affinities between the two men's attitudes toward black artistic consciousness. Here Hughes confesses that it was during his early visit to Africa that he had become conscious of his role as a poet. The text of the brief interview follows:

This American writer is unique inasmuch as he is concerned with blacks, with everything related to blacks.

"Now it's in vogue, you know," he explains. "But I've been interested in these things for a long time. Before, in my country Russia was in vogue. About seven years ago Americans only read Russian literature. It was the rage. Today nothing interests them as much as blacks. When this fad passes on I think the next thing will be Indians, everything related to the indigenous peoples of the continent."

Hughes's Spanish is not the best, but he makes marvelous use of it. He always is able to say what he wants, and he always has something to say.

"I really should have been a professional man. My family wanted me to be a doctor, a lawyer, or an engineer. But to tell the truth, the only thing I've done since I was fourteen was write poetry—and poetry doesn't sell for much. Let me put it this way, this was my way of reacting to the misery of poverty, to the terrible condition in which blacks live in my country.

"After spending a year at Columbia University, I took a trip

around the world, free of all worries and living on the fringe of
society. My first job was as a field worker; later I worked as a
waiter on a ship and as a sailor, too. This was the period that I
was in Africa."

"Africa?"

"Yes, I've been to Dakar, Nigeria, Loanda. It was in that part
of the world that my soul was strengthened in its love for black
people—a feeling that I will never lose. In contact with these
gentle people, whose arms were severed by the Belgians and who
were made to slave in the jungles by the French as the journalist
Alberto Londres has revealed, I realized that I had to be their
friend, their voice, their leader, their poet. My greatest ambition
is to be the poet of the blacks. The black poet. Do you
understand?"

Yes, I certainly understand and I feel that the poem which
opens this man's first book of poetry springs from the depths of
my soul: "I am a Negro/Black as the night is Black/Black like
the depths of my Africa."

"From Africa," Hughes continued," I went to Europe. I
visited Paris, Milan, Venice, Genoa. I suffered a lot. I worked at
the most menial jobs. I learned the troubles of the poor
firsthand. I worked my way back to the States and arrived
without a nickel to my name. I landed one cold winter afternoon
in New York, broke and down on my luck. That night I went to
Harlem. Luckily my poetry caught on. Some friends helped me
and in 1926 I published my first book, *The Weary Blues,* which
contained my black poems, my 'jazz poems,' written for that
kind of music, sea poems which recalled my barefoot days on
board ship in Africa and Europe and my love poems, because I
also had time for love."

"And afterwards?"

"Then my second book of poems, *Fine Clothes to the Jew,*
appeared. It has blues and spiritual poems, both reflections of
popular black American music and also several race and work
poems. Poems which always deal with my people. My latest
book will come out in August. It's a novel called *Not Without
Laughter,* which describes the life of a black family in the
Midwest and in which I try to show how that, in spite of their

enormous suffering and struggle against racial prejudice, laughter often lessens their burden. The manuscript is in the hands of the editor."

"How do you perceive," I asked him, "the racial problem in the United States with reference to blacks? Is a solution near at hand? I would like to know your opinion."

The poet smiles, plays with his school ring with its glistening emblem, and finally answers:

"Listen, I'm not a trained sociologist, I've never had any training in that field, I'm simply a poet. I live among my people; I love them and the way they're treated hurts me deeply so I sing their blues and I translate their sorrows, I make their troubles go away. And I do this like my people do, with their same ease. You know I've never bothered to learn the rules of versification. I'm one of those lucky people who has never written a sonnet. I write what comes from within. I sing it the same way old people do. I don't study the black man. I 'feel' him."

Finishing this idea, he goes on:

"My only aspiration is to make sure blacks don't lose their openness and forget their origins. I think white civilization can destroy black heritage by dressing blacks in white clothes which will never really be theirs. Of course there are blacks who don't agree with me because they think my poems are only about poor people and low life while they're busy playing at being aristocrats, imitating their old masters. But what can you do?"

Hughes is very concerned about blacks in Cuba. Wherever he goes he asks about blacks.

"Do blacks come to this cafe? Do they let blacks play in this orchestra? Aren't there black artists here? Boy, I'd like to go to a black dance hall."

So I took him to a black dance hall. From the very minute he enters, he acts like he's possessed with the spirit of our people.

"My people!" he exclaims.

For a long time he stands next to the band which is wildly playing a Cuban *son* and is gradually overcome by this new spirit within him.

Afterwards, while he looks at a black man dancing rhythmically he exclaims with an air of insatisfaction:

"I'd like to be black. Really black, truly black."[49]

Guillén's interview was followed in a matter of days by a brief reference to Hughes in Pedro Marco's article "Canción de la Calle" ("Street Song") published in the *Diario de la Marina* on 16 March. As critics have been careful to point out,[50] Hughes's early contact with Guillén was to have a profound effect on the young Cuban, who had not yet written his landmark collection *Motivos de son (Son motifs)*. Guillén sent a copy of the book to Hughes, who replied with a letter of praise on 17 July 1930:

> Your *Motivos de Son* is really great! The poems are very Cuban and very good. I'm glad you wrote them and that they have been so successful. I was in Washington and a young Cuban helped me to translate the poem. I thought "Tu no sabe inglé" with its "entrai guan" was really funny. I thought "Negro Bembón" was funny too. I don't know which poem I liked the best. I guess I liked them all. "Ayé me dijeron negro" is real cute. "Si tú supiera" is good too, but I don't understand what "songoro cosongo" means nor did my Cuban friend in Washington. Explain it to me.[51]

Another result of their friendship was a series of translations of Guillén's poetry into English carried out by Hughes and Ben Frederic Carruthers, a professor of Spanish at Howard University. Their *Cuba Libre: Poems by Nicolás Guillén* was the first book-length translation of his poems into English.[52]

If the early comments by Guillén and Fernández de Castro served to introduce Hughes to the Latin American public, the opinions of the Cuban critics Ramón Vasconcelos and Regino E. Boti firmly cemented the American poet's reputation, if only from a negative perspective. The journalist Vasconcelos, in his article "*Motivos de son*" ("*Son Motifs*"), referred to Hughes by indirectly denying any relationship between the Cuban *son* and the "Blues." He wrote that "Cuba is not the North American South nor is the *son* the 'Blues,' just as the guitar is not the banjo. Neither better nor worse, it is a different matter."[53] However, Guillén disagreed with Vasconcelos and refuted him in an article entitled "*Sones and soneros*" ("*Sones* and players of *sones*")[54] published in *El país* on 12 June 1930. In another important study of Guillén's poetry by Regino E. Boti, "La poesía cubana de Nicolás Guillén" ("The Cuban Poetry of Nicolás Guillén") Hughes's name appeared again. Much like Vasconcelos, Boti denied any literary relationship between Hughes and Guillén:

> . . . The tone of Nicolás Guillén's poetry being strange to Cuba, there was the necessity among critics to search abroad in order to assign him a heritage. And they found one in Langston Hughes, and I now answer—questioning in turn—those who have asked me in person what literary relationship exists between Hughes and Guillén? In the lyrical aspect, none. Just as a Yankee and a Cuban have nothing in common, the two poets are different, and so are their poems. The muse of Hughes waits. Guillén's cries out. Given this, why insist on a false heritage?[55]

This polemic, which focused on the aesthetic values and origins of black poetry, could not fail to enhance Hughes's growing recognition in the Hispanic world.

In the spring of 1931 with the money he had received from the Harmon Gold Award for Literature, Hughes made a trip to Cuba and Haiti accompanied by his friend Zell Ingram. By now he was a well-known figure in Cuban artistic circles. In fact Hughes had already published a short note on the black Cuban sculptor, Ramos Blanco, in *Opportunity* one year earlier and had been actively corresponding with his Cuban friends since his last trip.[56] His arrival in April 1931 was signaled by an essay in the *Diario de la Marina*, "El poeta Langston Hughes nos visita de nuevo" ("The Poet Langston Hughes Visits Us Again"). The author was careful to note the relationship between Hughes's art and black Caribbean literature: "His own new black art requires a special new world. The black man of the Antilles is virgin wax which he will shape."[57] In September 1931, Gustavo Urrutia again called attention to Hughes's role in the sphere of black literature in his "El paraíso de los negros" ("Black Paradise"),[58] where he announces Hughes's plans to visit Haiti.

As with his earlier experiences in Mexico, Hughes captured his impressions of Cuba in poetry. For example, in June 1933 he published a somewhat stylized reflection on Cuban high life called "Havana Dreams" in *Opportunity*. This poem, which incorporates a Spanish phrase (¿Quien sabe?) in its last line, is a good example of Hughes's success with verse miniatures:

Havana Dreams

The dream is a cocktail at Sloppy Joe's—
(Maybe—nobody knows.)

The dream is the road to Batabano.
(But nobody knows if that is so.)

Perhaps the dream is, only her face—
Perhaps it's a fan of silver lace—
Or maybe the dream's a Vedado rose—
(*Quien sabe?* Who really knows?)[59]

There is, however, a marked difference in theme and tone between his Mexican writings and those that date from his trips to the Caribbean. Whereas in the former the Hispanic element served merely as a colorful backdrop, in the latter Hughes has become conscious that the black experience, with its attendant feelings of alienation and subjugation, is an international phenomenon. He devoted several pages of *I Wonder as I Wander*[60] to describing racial discrimination in Havana and published a short story, "Little Old Spy,"[61] in *Esquire* in which he depicted the racist policies of the Machado dictatorship. In May 1931, Hughes published "To the Little Fort, San Lázaro, On the Ocean Front Havana" in *New Masses*. A bitter attack on economic imperialism, the poem prefigures the radical assault on society which Guillén would undertake in *West Indies Ltd.* (1934) and at the same time is vaguely reminiscent of the early social protest poetry of Hughes's Mexican friend Carlos Pellicer, poetry with which he was no doubt familiar. The text of the poem reads:

Watch tower once for pirates
That sailed the sun-bright seas—
Red pirates, great romantics,
    Drake,
    De Plan,
    El Grillo,
Against such as these
Years and years ago
You served quite well—

> When time and ships were slow.
> But now,
> Against a pirate called
> THE NATIONAL CITY BANK
> What can you do alone?
> Would it not be
> Just as well you tumbled down,
> Stone by helpless stone?[62]

III. Haiti

From Cuba Hughes traveled to Haiti, where he spent about two months in Cap Haitien. On his way back to the United States via Cuba he briefly met the novelist Jacques Roumain whose novel, *Gouverneurs de la Rosée* Hughes later translated with the help of Mercer Cook and René Piquion under the title *Masters of the Dew.*[63] Although his stay in Haiti was brief, the experience was not without importance to Hughes from both a creative and an intellectual point of view. It seems to have intensified his outrage at the treatment of blacks, a feeling reflected in articles published in *New Masses, The Crisis,* and *The New Republic.*[64] His first comment on his Haitian travels was a brief protest note published in *New Masses* in July 1931:

A Letter from Haiti

Haiti is a hot, tropical little country, all mountains and sea; a lot of marines, mulatto politicians, and a world of black people without shoes—who catch hell.

The Citadel, twenty miles away on a mountain top, is a splendid lonely monument to the genius of a black king—Christophe. Stronger, vaster, and more beautiful than you could possibly imagine. . . . it stands in futile ruin now, the iron cannon rusting, the bronze one turning green, the great passages and deep stairways alive with bats, while the planes of the United States Marines hum daily overhead. . . .[65]

Langston Hughes

Cap Haitien, Haiti.

The following October he wrote a brief essay "People Without

Shoes" for the same magazine in which he denounced the economic
rape of Haiti by the forces of the American occupation:

> The American Occupation lives in the best houses. The officials
> of the National City Bank, New York, keep their heavy-jawed
> portraits in the offices of the Banque d'Haiti. And because black
> hands have touched the earth, gathered in the fruits, and loaded
> ships, somebody—across the class and color lines—many
> somebodies become richer and wiser, educate their children to
> read and write, to travel, to be ambitious, to be superior, to
> create armies, and to build banks. Somebody wears coats and
> shoes.[66]

The same theme was echoed in "White Shadows in a Black Land"
which appeared in the *Crisis* in May 1932. Hughes wrote: "The dark-
skinned little Republic, then, has its hair caught in the white fingers
of unsympathetic foreigners, and the Haitian people live today under
a sort of military dictatorship backed by American guns. They are
not free."[67]

The influence of Haiti in his work was not entirely political,
however. In 1932, in collaboration with Arna Bontemps, he wrote an
idyllic novella for children entitled *Popo and Fifina*[68] and authored a
play, *Emperor of Haiti: An Historical Drama,* which was performed
by the New York City Opera Company in 1949 under the title
Troubled Island.

IV. Spain

Hughes's most intense and sustained relationship with the Hispanic world was probably the six-month period during which he
served as a correspondent for the Afro-American newspapers
covering the events of the Spanish Civil War. En route to Spain
Hughes first stopped in Paris in July 1937, where he delivered a
passionate speech to the Second International Writers Congress in
which he linked fascism with racism:

> Members of the Second International Writers Congress, com-
> rades, and people of Paris: I come from a land whose democracy

from the very beginning has been tainted with race prejudice born of slavery, and whose richness has been poured through the narrow channels of greed into the hands of the few. I come to the Second International Writers Congress representing my country, America, but most especially the Negro peoples of America, and the poor peoples of America—because I am both a Negro and poor. And that combination of color and of poverty gives me the right then to speak for the most oppressed group in America, that group that has known so little of American democracy, the fifteen million Negroes who dwell within our borders.[69]

He lingered in Paris renewing his friendship with Nicolás Guillén and Jacques Roumain before leaving by train for Barcelona with Guillén. After traveling to Barcelona and then to Valencia, Hughes continued to Madrid where he took up residence at the Alianza de Intelectuales. It was here in particular that the poet met many important writers of the thirties. His own work was soon translated into Spanish by the Spanish poet Miguel Alejandro[70] and he himself began with the help of Rafael Alberti and Manuel Altolaguirre the first draft of a translation of Federico García Lorca's *Romancero Gitano* under the title *Gypsy Ballads*.[71] During his stay at the Alianza Hughes met two important Cuban writers: Alejo Carpentier, who had written essays on *Négritude* during the twenties,[72] and the short story writer Lino Novás Calvo.

Hughes was extraordinarily active as a writer during his stay in Spain. In addition to the series of articles he wrote for the *Baltimore Afro-American,* he published a number of poems about the Spanish Civil War. In these poems Hughes formally reveals himself a spokesman for the downtrodden of the world. His earlier attempts to decry racism and prejudice in poems from *Crisis* and *The Weary Blues* re-emerge here as a universalized assault on fascism and war. One of the first of these pieces, "Letter from Spain Addressed to Alabama,"[73] reflects Hughes's growing concern with the historical consciousness peculiar to black men. His contacts with Guillén of Cuba and Roumain of Haiti seem to have intensified an awareness of *Négritude* first expressed in "Negro" which appeared in the *Crisis* in January 1922, and which Guillén recalled in his interview with Hughes. "Letter from Spain" a nine-stanza poem composed in the form of a rhymed letter was written, Hughes explains, to try to express the feelings of the black soldiers of the International Brigade about fighting the colonial Moors—victims themselves of the oppression in North Africa. Stylistically it reveals the lineal form and tone of simple statement which he first elaborated in *The Weary Blues*. Midway in the poem his persona then turns his eyes to Africa and underscores both the economic and racial ties between him and his Moorish brother:

> And as he lay there dying
> In a village we had taken,
> I looked across to Africa
> And seed foundations shakin'.
>
> Cause if a free Spain wins this war,
> The colonies, too, are free—
> Then something wonderful'll happen
> To them Moors as dark as me.[74]

Perhaps the most widely known poem he wrote on the theme was "Song of Spain," which was published in English in *A New Song* by the International Workers Order in 1938.[75] The same year it was anthologized in Nancy Cunard and Pablo Neruda's edition of *Deux Poèmes* and received wide circulation in Spain.[76] As early as September 1937, Novás Calvo was commenting on the poem in an article in Madrid's *Ayuda* entitled "El que cantó Harlem, canta China y España" ("He Who Sang of Harlem, Sings of China and Spain"), and it was also discussed in the Mexican journal *Ruta*.[77] Using his most familiar stylistic devices of repetition and elementary diction, Hughes constructs a poem which gradually builds to a dramatic crescendo. More than a denunciation of fascism, it is a personal plea for the workers of the world to refuse to participate in war:

> I must drive the bombers out of Spain!
> I must drive the bombers out of the world!
> I must take the world for my own again—
>
> A worker's world
> Is the song of Spain.

The denunciation of war per se was indeed the focus of two visually graphic poems ("Air Raid Barcelona," "Moonlight in Valencia: Civil War") and an unpublished poem which begins "Put out the lights and stop the clocks."[78] The first poem begins with a powerful synesthetic image—"Black smoke of sound / Curls against the midnight sky"—is vaguely reminiscent of García Lorca in its emphasis on contrasting visual images. In poems such as "Tomorrow's Seed" and "Hero-International Brigade"[79] Hughes focuses on the heroism of the black soldiers who fought in the Civil War by, once again, equating their fight against fascism with a step in the battle for universal freedom.

The decades following his return from Spain saw Hughes's reputation grow exponentially. Many of his major works were translated into Spanish. In 1944, for example, Luis Rivand translated Hughes's autobiography, *The Big Sea,* with the title *El inmenso mar* (Buenos Aires: Editorial Lautaro) and the following year Nestor R. Ortís Oderigo prepared a Spanish version of the novel *Not Without Laughter* (*Pero con risas,* Buenos Aires: Editorial Futuro). Julio Galer published an anthology of his poems under the title *Poemas* (Buenos Aires: Lautaro) in 1952; translated *Mulatto* (*Mulato: Drama en dos actos,* Buenos Aires: Editorial Quetzal) in 1954; *Laughing to Keep from Crying* (*Riendo por no llorar,* Buenos Aires: Ediciones Siglo Veinte), in 1959; and *I Wonder as I Wander* (*Yo viajo por el mundo encantado,* Buenos Aires: Compañía General Fabril) the same year. Five of Hughes's poems were anthologized in the influential collection of black poetry edited by Emilio Ballagas (*Mapa de la poesía negra americana,* Buenos Aires: Editorial Pleamar, 1946) and a translation of "Blues I'm Playing" appeared in Lenka Franulic's *Antología del cuento norteamericano* (Santiago: Ediciones Ercilla, 1943). Aside from these, there were numerous translations of individual poems and short stories. It should be further noted that in 1957 Hughes published a translation of the poetry of the Nobel Laureate, Gabriela Mistral: *Selected Poems of Gabriela Mistral* (Bloomington: Indiana University Press).

Hispanic critics and scholars also began to attend to Hughes's work. Eugenio Florit included Hughes in his *Antología de la poesía norteamericana contemporánea* (Washington: Unión panamericana, 1955) and Gastón Figueira[80] studied the poet in an essay in the *Revista Iberoamericana* ("Dos poetas norteamericanos: I

Sinclair Lewis. II Langston Hughes," 18, January-September 1953, pp. 401–404). His broad popularity in the Hispanic world is more recently reflected in a proposal in the Venezuelan newspaper, *El Universal* (November 1960) that Hughes be considered for the Nobel Prize in Literature. After his death in 1967, eulogies appeared in important Hispanic magazines. Nicolás Guillén, Concha Zardoya, Andrés Henestrosa, Ernesto Mejía Sánchez, José Luis González, and others called attention to the poet's death and to his work.[81]

A number of observations can be drawn from a study of Hughes's relationship to the Spanish-speaking world. We have seen how his reputation grew as a result of two important contacts: Pellicer and the *Contemporáneos* in Mexico and Guillén and the poets of *Négritude* in the Caribbean. It was Hughes's stay in Spain, however, that catalyzed his poetic vision, for it was here that he renewed his contacts with Pellicer and Guillén and wrote some of his most important poems of social protest. Hughes's denunciation of the tragedy of Spain was contemporary with and parallel to the activities of the foremost poets of the Hispanic world: Pablo Neruda, César Vallejo, Nicolás Guillén, and Octavio Paz. While these writers described the terrible disintegration of their native heritage, Hughes decried the evils of fascism and wrote of the common bonds which link all black men—a theme which emerges as the matrix of thought in his poetic vision. It was his contacts with the Spanish language and culture which reinforced and gave substance to his concept of *Négritude*. Furthermore, Hughes's acquaintance with the Hispanic world was more than a superficial encounter; it was a deeply-felt symbiotic relationship. His travels in the Spanish-speaking world not only provided the thematic underpinnings of some of his best short stories (*Spanish Blood* and *Tragedy at the Bath* are two examples) but they allowed him to deftly incorporate Spanish words and phrases in many of his poems and works of prose fiction.

While it is easy to understand Hughes's enormous popularity in those lands whose national poets have been vehemently anti-American, this does not detract from nor diminish his universal appeal as a poet of simple truths. The impressive reputation of Langston Hughes outside the sphere of North American literature is but another link in the chain of evidence for his stature as an international poet.

[1]Conrad Kent Rivers, "A Preface to . . . for All Things Black and Beautiful," *Negro Digest* 16 (September 1967): 32.

[2]For a good general study of Hughes see James A. Emanuel, *Langston Hughes* (New York: Twayne, 1967). Slighter but of some interest is François Dodat, *Langston Hughes* (Paris: Seghers, 1964) and Milton Meltzer, *Langston Hughes: A Biography* (New York: Apollo, 1972). The most complete bibliography is: Donald C. Dickinson, *A Bio-Bibliography of Langston Hughes, 1902-1967* (Hamden, Conn.: Shoe String Press, 1967). See especially "Foreign Reception," pp. 117-19.

[3]For a briefer treatment of this theme see my article "Presencia y evaluación de Langston Hughes en Hispanoamérica," *Revista de la Comunidad Latinoamericana de Escritores* 15 (1974): 16-21. A briefer version of this present essay appeared in *Comparative Literature Studies,* 8 (September 1976): 254-269.

[4]Nancy Cunard, "Three Negro Poets," *Left Review* 2 (October 1937): 530.

[5]Cited in D. C. Dickinson, *A Bio-Bibliography,* p. 118.

[6]*Yo también soy América,* ed. and trans. Herminio Ahumada (México: Novaro, 1968).

[7]Ernesto Mejía Sánchez, review of *Yo también soy América, Amaru, Revista de Artes y Ciencias,* (April-June 1968): 95: "Consideró esa empresa como la cumbre de su carrera, pareja a la publicación de sus *Selected poems* de este año."

[8]For a brief comment on Hughes's travels in the Spanish-speaking world see José Ferrer, "Langston Hughes: El cantor de las penas de la raza de color ha tenido contacto con la cultura hispánica," *Repertorio Americano* 49 (1955): 104-106.

[9]Hughes wrote the following in his autobiography, *The Big Sea* (New York: Knopf, 1942), p. 15: "When I was about five or six years old, my father and mother decided to go back together. They had separated shortly after I was born, because my father wanted to go away to another country, where a colored man could get ahead and make money quicker, and my mother did not want to go. My father went to Cuba, and then to Mexico, where there wasn't any color line, or any Jim Crow. He finally sent for us, so we went there, too."

[10]Ibid., p. 19.

[11]"The one of my poems that has perhaps been most often reprinted in anthologies, was written on the train during this trip to Mexico when I was feeling very bad. It's called 'The Negro Speaks of Rivers' and was written just outside St. Louis, as the train rolled toward Texas." (Ibid., p. 54.)

[12]Mary White Ovington, *Portraits in Color* (New York: Viking, 1927) pp. 197-98.

[13]Hughes, "Mexican Market Woman," *The Crisis* 5 (December 1922): 68-70.

[14]Quoted in Drewey W. Gunn, *American and British Writers in Mexico, 1556-1973* (Austin: University of Texas Press, 1974), p. 83.

[15]*The Brownies Book* was published monthly from January 1920 to December 1921.

[16]Hughes, "Mexican Games," *Brownies Book* 2 (January 1921): 18.

[17]Hughes, "In a Mexican City," Ibid. 2 (April 1921): 102–105.

[18]Hughes, "Up to the Crater of an Old Volcano," Ibid. 2 (December 1921: 334–38.

[19]Hughes, "The Virgin of Guadalupe," *Crisis* 23 (December 1921): 77. Hughes later published "Love in Mexico" in *Opportunity* 8 (April 1940): 107–108.

[20]Drewey Gunn, *American and British Writers,* p. 84.

[21]For a discussion of Pellicer's involvement in black poetry, see my essay, "Nicolás Guillén and Carlos Pellicer: A Case of Literary Parallels," *Latin American Literary Review* 3 (spring-summer 1975): 77–87.

[22]See my essay "European and North American Writers in *Contemporáneos,*" *Comparative Literature Studies* 8 (December 1971): 338–46. The following poems were translated: "I, Too," "Poem," "Prayer," and "Suicide's Note."

[23]Salvador Novo, "Notas sobre la poesía de los negros en los Estados Unidos," *Contemporáneos* 11 (September-October 1931): 197–200. Ortiz de Montellano had earlier written some short poems on black themes in "Motivos negros," Ibid. 2 (October 1928): 111–12. The translation here is excerpted from my "Notes on Black Poetry" *Review '76,* no. 17 (spring 1976): pp. 21–22.

[24]For a description of the journal see Boyd G. Carter, *Historia de la literatura hispanoamericana a través de sus revistas* (Mexico, 1968), 1: 105–07 and *Las revistas literarias de Hispanoamérica* (Mexico, 1959), pp. 98–99. The former contains an extensive bibliography on other vanguard reviews (pp. 109–111) and on vanguardism in general (pp. 246–51). Also of interest is Merlin Forster's "La revista *Contemporáneos* ¿Hacia una mexicanidad universal?" *Hispanófila* 17 (January 1963): 117–22.

[25]At about the same time Jorge Luis Borges published a translation of the "Negro Speaks of Rivers" and "Our Land" in *Sur* 1 (fall 1931): 164–69. The translations were followed by this note: "With Countee Cullen (whose wise, tragic, and delicate art is difficult to capture) and with the untranslatable Jean Toomer, Langston Hughes is one of the most important North American poets. He was born in 1902 in Joplin, Missouri. He has published *The Weary Blues,* 1925, and *Fine Clothes to the Jew,* 1927."

("Con Countée Cullen (cuyo arte delicado, trágico y sabio parece de difícil versión) y con el también intraducible Jean Toomer, Langston Hughes es de los poetas negros norteamericanos más destacados. Nació en 1902, en Joplin, Missouri. Ha publicado *The Weary Blues,* 1925, y *Fine Clothes to the Jew,* 1927.")

[26]Rafael Lozano, "Langston Hughes: El poeta afroestadounidense," *Crisol, Revista de Crítica* 5 (March 1931): p. 227: "La poesía de L. H. es eminentemente espontánea. Tiene esa natural negligencia, nacida de la emoción de que nos habla Charles Guerin. Lo mismo canta a las prostitutas negras de Harlem que a una placera de México . . . Pero en todos sus versos se advierte la nota personal, la observación directa, desliteraturizada, vivida intensamente y sentida hasta el paroxismo. No es suprarealista ni mallar-

meano, ni siquiera ha sufrido la influencia de Baudelaire, del Baudelaire de *Albatros* y del amor por lo exótico. Es un canto primitivo, como todos los de su raza, que se expresa en ritmos propios, un poco sincopados, como la música del jazz."

[27]See Hughes's autobiography, *I Wonder As I Wander* (New York: Rinehart, 1956), pp. 285-300.

[28]Ibid., p. 291.

[29]Andrés Henestrosa recalled his days with Hughes in two short articles: "Un poeta negro," *Novedades,* 1 June 1967, p. 4, cols. 3-4; "Un extraño suceso," Ibid., 8 June 1967, p. 4, cols. 3-4. See also "Un poeta negro, amigo de México," in *Yo también soy América,* trans. and ed. Herminio Ahumada, (Mexico, Novaro 1968), pp. 7-9. During this period Hughes was active as a translator. He translated a short story by Antonio Acevedo Escobedo, "Fire in the Rain," *Rocky Mountain Review* 2 (spring 1938): 8, poems by Francisca (Nellie Campobello) in Dudley Fitts (ed.) *Anthology of Contemporary Latin American Poetry* (New York: New Directions, 1947), pp. 213-19, and poetry in Miguel Covarrubias's *Mexico South* (New York: Knopf, 1947), pp. 18-20, 31-35, 312-18, 330-35 (cited in Gunn, *American and British Writers in Mexico,* p. 86).

[30]José Antonio Fernández de Castro, "Langston Hughes, poeta militante negro," *El Nacional,* 3 March 1935, p. 1:
"Por ser tan hondamente popular es tan artística la poesía de L. H. Expresando por su boca los dolores que sufren sus hermanos de raza, cumple su deber de hombre artista. Allí donde hay una tristeza negra, producida por la injusticia del blanco, allí encontraremos a Langston Hughes que la recogerá en sus cantos para lanzarla al mundo. Pero como la naturaleza del negro es tan fuerte, tan digna de ser imitada ¡que digo de ser imitada!, de ser recogida e incorporada a nuestro carácter popular, el negro no se limita a quejarse. Sabe reírse de sus penas. Y como Langston es negro tamién se ríe. En sus poemas también hay risa y color y luz y sonido y esplendor. Que todo eso hay en alma negra."

[31]Luis Cardoza y Aragón, "Langston Hughes, el poeta de los negros," *El Nacional,* 17 March 1935, p. 6.

[32]"*Nostalgia of Death* concludes with five poems grouped under the heading, 'Nostaligias'; of these, all with the exception of 'Death in Tenths' appeared in final form in the 1938 edition. 'North Carolina Blues' seems strangely out of place; dedicated to Langston Hughes, it is an unfruitful effort to assimilate Hughes' jazz-influenced rhythms and is interesting only because of several unusually sensual images and Villaurrutia's concise comment on Jim Crowism." (Frank Dauster, *Xavier Villaurrutia,* New York: Twayne, 1971, p. 52.)

[33]See "Música," *Letras de México* 2 (June 1939): 4. The note reads: "Silvestre Revueltas prepara 'Cinco Canciones' para piano sólo con textos de Langston Hughes y otros poetas. El mismo autor dió ya por terminado su 'Poema Sinfónico sobre España', que probablemente se estrene durante el curso del año."

[34]With reference to his first meeting in 1947 with Hughes, González Flores

wrote in *Una pareja de tantos* (Mexico: Yolotepec, 1950), p. 245: I had never seen Langston Hughes before that night. My admiration for him grew from the reading of some poems of his in the Sunday supplement of some paper. Afterwards, occasionally I heard part of his autobiography *The Big Sea* read at literary gatherings. Later, at the end of World War II, I translated *Freedom's Plow,* whose original English version had been read on the air by Paul Muni on the *Red Azul.*"

["Nunca, antes de aquella noche, habíamos vista a Langston Hughes. Mi admiración por él nació de la lectura de poemas sueltos en las páginas dominicales de algún periódico. Después, ocasionalmente, en una reunión literaria escuché parte de su libro autobiográfico *El inmenso mar,* sinopsis de sus confesiones de vagabundo. Más tarde, en las postrimerías de la segunda Gran Guerra, le traduje *El arado de la libertad,* cuyo original en inglés—que había sido radiado en la *Red Azul* por el actor Paul Muni, . . . "] Part of this essay was reprinted in "una visita a Langston Hughes," *El Nacional,* 12 September 1948, p. 13.

[35]See "El arado de la libertad," *América: Tribuna de la Democracia,* no. 52 (October 1946): 63–70; "La balada de Harry Moore," *Revista Mexicana de Cultura* (suplemento dominical de *El Nacional*) no. 311 (15 March 1953): 5; and "Yo también canto América," *Siempre: Presencia de México,* no. 729 (14 June 1967): ix.

[36]"El gran poeta negro norteamericano Langston Hughes," *Nivel,* no. 31 (25 July 1961) 5: xv.

[37]Germán Pardo García in *Nivel,* no. 158: 6.

"Digno émulo de Luther King, de Robenson, . . . Langston Hughes es uno de los más gloriosos precursores de la emancipación de una esclavitud que todavía existe en América y en otros lugares del mundo, . . .

"Langston Hughes lanzó, desde sus inicios, un grito de alarma que continúa reproduciéndose en el seno de la conciencia de una raza dolorida, que busca su definitiva redención: 'I am, too, America . . .'." Pardo García has also referred to Hughes in two poems: "Bosques humanos" in *Apolo Thermador* (Mexico: Libros de México, 1971), pp. 187–91 and "Negrura del genesis" in *Genesis* (Mexico: Libros de México, 1968), pp. 29–30.

[38]Abigael Bohórquez, "Carta abierta a Langston Hughes," *La Palabra y el Hombre* 6 (January-March 1962): 147–52.

[39]Leopoldo Ayala, "Réquiem para la tumba de un cuerpo," *La Poesía joven de México* (Mexico: Siglo Veinte, 1968), pp. 40–42.

[40]Letter from Antonio Acevedo Escobedo, 16 August 1975.

"Un organismo izquierdista de la época del régimen de Cárdenas. Se puso énfasis en situar a Langston dentro de esa tendencia, al margen de que en su poesía prevalezca un sentido estrictamente universal, como usted lo apunta."

[41]See "El gran poeta negro Langston Hughes regresa a los EE.UU," *Nivel,* no. 46 (25 October 1962): 6. See also José Luis González, "La muerte de dos grandes escritores norteamericanos," *Siempre: Presencia de México,* no. 729 (14 June 1967): v–ix.

[42]Hughes, "Powder White Faces," *Common Ground* (New York: Hill and Wang, 1963), pp. 147–53.

[43]See Fernández de Castro, "Poeta militante negro," p. 1.

[44]José Antonio Fernández de Castro, "Yo, Tambien . . . ," *Social* (September 1928): 28.

[45]Hughes wrote in *The Big Sea*, p. 324:
"That winter I had been in Cuba looking for a Negro composer to write an opera with me, using genuinely racial motifs. The lady on Park Avenue thought that Amadeo Roldan might do, or Arturo Cartulo. I could not find Cartulo, and Roldan said he wasn't a Negro. But Miguel Covarrubias had given me a letter to José Antonio Fernández de Castro, person extraordinary of this or any other world. And José Antonio saw to it that I had a rumba of a good time and met everybody, Negro, white and mulatto, of any interest in Havana—from the drummers at Marianao to the society artist and editor of *Social*, Masaguer.
"But I came back to New York with no Negro composer who could write an opera."

[46]See Hughes, *I Wonder As I Wander*, p. 8.

[47]José Antonio Fernández de Castro, "Presentación de Langston Hughes," *Revista de la Habana* 1, 3 (March 1930): 368: "En la obra lírica de L. H.—como en toda la de Countee Cullen, Walter F. White, Jessie Fauscet, Claude Mac-Kay, para no nombrar más que a los más representativos escritores de la raza negra en los Estados Unidos—está patente un vigoroso orgullo racial, una combatividad desconocida hasta el momento presente por parte de los productores intelectuales de esa raza. Su técnica es moderna y su sensibilidad alcanza matices personalísimos que lo hacen destacar con propios lineamientos dentro del complicado panorama que es la contemporánea producción poética en los Estados Unidos." It should be pointed out that Fernández Castro also published a translation from *Not Without Laughter*, "Oye muchacho," *Revista de La Habana* 1, 7/8 (July-August 1930): 77–84.

[48]Guillén recalled his early association with Hughes in "Le souvenir de Langston Hughes," *Présence Africaine* 64 (October-December 1967): 34–37. Also see Lino Novás Calvo, "Cuba Literaria," *Gaceta Literaria*, Año 2, no. 118 (15 November 1931): 3.

[49]Nicholás Guillén, "Conversación con Langston Hughes," *Diario de la Marina*, 9 March 1930, p. 6.

[50]See the excellent study of David Arthur McMurray, "Dos negros en el Nuevo Mundo: Notas sobre el 'americanismo' del Langston Hughes y la Cubanía de Nicolás Guillén," *Casa de las Américas*, 14 (January-February 1974): 122–28 as well as Enrique Noble, "Aspectos étnicos y sociales de la poesía mulata latinoamericana," *Revista Bimestre Cubana* 40 (January-June 1958): 166–79 and "Nicolás Guillén y Langston Hughes" *Nueva Revista Cubana* (Havana: Editora del Consejo Nacional de Cultura, 1962) pp. 3–47. Also of importance are the briefer comments of José Antonio Portuondo in *Bosquejo histórico de las letras cubanas* (Havana: Editora del Ministerio de Educación, 1962) p. 63 and Cintio Vitier, *Lo cubano en la poesía* (La Habana: Ucar García y Cía, 1958), pp. 350–351.

[51]The text of the letter is cited in Angel Augier, *Nicolás Guillén: Notas*

para un estudio biográfico-crítico, 2 vols. (Santa Clara, Cuba: Universidad Central de las Villas, 1965) I: 139–40:

"¡Hombre! ¡Qué formidable tu *Motivos de Son*! Son poemas muy cubanos y muy buenos. Me alegro que tú los has escrito y que han tenido tanto éxito . . . Estuve yo en Washington y un joven cubano allí me ayudó a traducir tus versos. ¡Qué risa me da *Tú no sabe inglé* con su 'etrai guan'! *Negro Bembón* también. Quién sabe cuál me gusta más. Me gustan todos. *Ayé me dijeron negro* es precioso. *Si tú supiera* también, pero no comprendo el 'sóngoro, cosongo, songo bé' (ni el cubano en Washington tampoco). Explícamelo."

[52]With reference to the translation of Guillén's poetry Ben Frederic Carruthers the cotranslator wrote: "Upon my return to Howard in 1941 I began my own translations and when I moved to New York in 1944 I met Langston again and began to compare notes. We found that a few but not many of our translations were of the same poem but that there were many which I had finished which Langston thought good enough to stand as they were and many others which Langston had completed without my having touched them. We collaborated completely on the final editing and polishing and Langston secured the publisher and the artist, Gar Bilbert." Quoted in John F. Matheus, "Langston Hughes as Translator," in *Langston Hughes Black Genius,* ed. Therman B. O'Daniel (New York: William Morrow, 1971), p. 165. Translations of Guillén's poetry by Hughes and Carruthers also appeared in *The Crisis,* 55 (November 1948): 336–37.

[53]Quoted in Fernando de Ortiz, "Motivos de son, por Nicolás Guillén," *Archivos del Folklore Cubano,* 5 (July-September 1930): 228.

"Cuba no es el sur yanqui ni el son es el 'blue', como la guitarra no es el banjo. Ni mejor ni peor. Asunto distinto."

[54]Cited in Fernando de Ortiz, Ibid., p. 231.

[55]Regino E. Boti, "La poesía cubana de Nicolás Guillén," *Revista Bimestre Cubana* 29 (May-June 1932): 352: " . . . Siendo el tono de la poesía de Nicolás Guillén extraño en Cuba, hubo necesidad en los pesquisidores de acudir al extranjero para propinarle un ancestro. Y lo hallaron en Langston Hughes, y ahora contesto—preguntando a mi vez—a los que de viva voz me lo han dicho aquí en la aldea: ¿qué parentesco literario existe entre Hughes y Guillén? En lo esencialmente lírico, ninguno. Lo mismo que nada hay de común entre un yanqui y un cubano en lo que cada uno tiene de peculiar . . . Los dos poetas difieren, y sus cantos. La musa de Hughes espera. La de Guillén reclama . . . Después de lo antecedente, ¿a qué insistir en lo de falso parentesco?"

[56]Hughes, "A Cuban Sculptor," *Opportunity,* 8 (November 1930): 334.

[57]Santos Alberto, "El poeta Langston Hughes nos visita de nuevo," *Diario de la Marina,* 8 April 1931, p. 2: "Su arte propio, nuevo, Negro requiere un mundo nuevo y propio. El negro antillano es cera virgin que van ellos a modelar."

[58]Gustavo Urrutia, "El Paraíso de los negros," *Diario de la Marina,* 27 September 1932, p. 2.

[59]Hughes, "Havana Dreams," *Opportunity* (June 1933): 181.

[60]Hughes, *I Wonder As I Wander,* pp. 7-14.

[61]Hughes, "Little Old Spy," *Esquire,* 2 (September 1934): 47, 150-152.

[62]Hughes, "To the Little Fort San Lázaro," *New Masses,* 10 (May 1931): 11.

[63]*Master of the Dew,* trans. Mercer Cook and Langston Hughes (New York: Reynal and Hitchcock, 1947). See Matheus, "Langston Hughes as Translator," pp. 167-69.

[64]See Hughes, "A Letter from Haiti," *New Masses,* 12 (July 1931): 9; "People Without Shoes," *Ibid.* 12 (October 1931): 12; "White Shadows in a Black Land," *The Crisis,* 41 (May 1932): 157; "An Appeal for Jacques Romain [sic]" *New Republic,* 81 (12 December 1934): 130; "Haiti: Mood for Maracas," *Ibid.,* 145 (25 September 1961): 22.

[65]Hughes, "A Letter from Haiti," p. 9.

[66]Hughes, "People without Shoes," p. 12.

[67]Hughes, "White Shadows in a Black Land," p. 157.

[68]Hughes, *Popo and Fifina,* Children of Haiti (New York: Macmillan 1932). See the comments of Lydia Filatova, "Langston Hughes: American Writer," *Soviet Literature* 20, no. 1 (1933): 99-107.

[69]Hughes, "Too Much of Race," in *Good Morning Revolution: Uncollected Writings of Social Protest,* ed. Faith Berry (New York: Lawrence Hill, 1973), p. 97.

[70]Miguel Alejandro, "Buenos días, Revolución" and "El Waldorf Astoria" in *Nueva Cultura* (January 1936): 6-9.

[71]See Matheus, "Langston Hughes as Translator," pp. 158-64. The Hughes translation was first published in the *Beloit Poetry Chapbook,* no. 1 (Fall 1951). It contains fifteen of the eighteen ballads in the original text. A note to the typescript reads: "First translated at the Alianza de Escritores in Madrid with the aid of Rafael Alberti and Manuel Altolaguirre. Revised in New York, July, 1945, with the aid of Miguel Covarrubias. Checked with the Lloyd, Spender, and Barea versions. Final Copy, July 20, 1945."

[72]For a description of their meeting see Klaus Mueller-Berg, *Alejo Carpentier: Estudio biográfico-crítico* (New York: Las Américas, 1972), pp. 27-28.

[73]Hughes, "Letter from Spain Addressed to Alabama," *Volunteer For Liberty: Organ of the International Brigades,* (15 November 1937): 3.

[74]Ibid., p. 3.

[75]An interesting observation about this poem was made by Professor Paul Rogers in a letter to this writer dated 23 July 1975: "Early on he wrote a poem to the Republic a manuscript copy of which he sent me. The poem you will recognize, I believe, for it is the one which begins with the opening lines of Cervantes *Quijote.* They were wrongly quoted, and I debated with myself whether to write of the error to Langston. Finally I did. He accepted the correction with the utmost grace, and later, when the poem was published, the quotation appeared in its correct form. This poem is now in the University of Texas Collection of material on the Spanish Civil War, housed in the Humanities Research Center and is considered one of the unique items of this remarkable collection."

[76]This poem originally appeared in January 1937, on unpaginated sheets

bearing the title *Deux poémes par Federico Garcia Lorca et Langston Hughes. Les poétes du monde défendent le peuple espagnol*—numéro trois—composé à la main par Nancy Cunard et Pablo Neruda, n.p.

[77]"Canto de España," *Ruta,* 1 (June 1928): 57.

[78]Hughes, *Esquire,* 10 (October 1938): 40; Thomas Yoseloff, ed. *Seven Poets in Search of an Answer* (New York: Bernard Ackerman, 1944), p. 51. The latter is an unpublished poem inscribed: "To Arthur Spingarn, Sincerely, Langston." It is located in the Arthur B. Spingarn Papers, Moorland-Spingarn Collection, Howard University Library.

[79]See Alvah Bessie, ed. *The Heart of Spain* (New York: Veterans of the Abraham Lincoln Brigade, Inc. 1952). pp. 325-26.

[80]Also see Gastón Figueira, "Langston Hughes, voz de una raza," *Sustancia: Revista de Cultura Superior* 12 (July 1942): 260-65.

[81]See Nicolás Guillén, "Le souvenir de Langston Hughes"; Concha Zardoya, "Dos poemas de Langston Hughes," *Insula,* nos. 248-49, (1967): 24; Andrés Henestrosa, "Un poeta negro"; Ernesto Mejía Sánchez, "Yo también soy América"; and José Luis González, "La muerte de dos grandes escritores norteamericanos."

Langston Hughes's Works
Translated into Spanish

The items in this bibliography are arranged alphabetically by English title. This is followed by the Spanish title, the name of the translator, and other facts of publication. In the case of poetry, the first line of the Spanish text is presented. For a list of translations into other languages readers should consult:

> Donald C. Dickinson, *A Bio-Bibliography of Langston Hughes, 1902-1967: Second Edition*[7] (Hamden, Conn: Shoe String Press, 1972).

The following abbreviations have been used in the text:

> *Antología* for Idelfonso Pereda Valdés, ed., *Antología de la poesía negra americana* (Santiago: Ediciones Ercilla, 1936).

> *Poemas* for *Poemas,* trans. Julio Galer (Buenos Aires: Editorial Lautaro, 1952).

> *Yo también* for Herminio Ahumada, ed. and trans., *Yo también Soy América* (México: Novaro, 1968).

The items in the bibliography of poetry follow the style of "An Index to Poem Titles" in *A Concordance to the Poetry of Langston Hughes,* comp. P. Mandelik and S. Schatt, (Detroit: Gale, 1975).

Translations of Prose and Drama

The Big Sea. El Inmenso Mar. trans. L. Rivaud. Buenos Aires: Lautaro, 1944. 308 pp.
"Dixie and Colored People." "Dixie y los pueblos de color."

Ultra: 13 (1943): 357–60.

I Wonder as I Wander. Yo viajo por un mundo encantado, trans.
      Julio Galer. Buenos Aires: Compañía General Fabril, 1959.
      417 pp.

Laughing to Keep from Crying. Riendo por no llorar, trans.
      Julio Galer. Buenos Aires: Ediciones Siglo Veinte, 1955. 184
      pp.

"Listen Boy." "¡Oye muchacho!" trans. J. J. Fernández de
      Castro. *La Revista de la Habana* nos. 7–8 (July-August 1930):
      77–84.

Mulatto. Mulato, Drama en dos actos, trans. Julio Galer.
      Buenos Aires: Editorial Quetzal, 1954. 57 pp.

Mulato, Drama en dos partes, trans. Alfonso Sastre. Madrid:
      Alfil. 79 pp.

Not Without Laughter. Pero con risas, trans. Néstor R. Ortís
      Oderigo. Buenos Aires: Editorial Futuro, 1945. 252 pp.

"Weary Blues." "Los Blues que estoy tocando," in *Antología*
      del cuento norteamericano. ed. L. Franulic. Santiago: Edi-
      ciones Ercilla, 1943, pp. 327–42.

"Los Blues que estoy tocando," in *Antología*
      del cuento americano contemporáneo. ed. Francisco Rojas
      González. México: Secretaría de Educación Pública, 1953,
      pp. 121–40.

Translations of Poetry

A House in Taos
      J. Galer, "Una casa en Taos," *Poemas,* pp. 91–92.
      "Lluvia"
A New Song
      H. Ahumada, "Una nueva canción," *Yo también,* p. 113.
      "Yo hablo en nombre de los millones de negros"
      Ibid., *Nivel* no. 158 (26 February 1976): 6.
Advertisement for Opening of the Waldorf Astoria
      Miguel Alejandro, "El Waldorf-Astoria," *Nueva Cultura*
      (January 1936): 9.
            Oh, Señor, Señor, yo nunca me he olvidado ni me/
            olvido de las calles de Harlem

J. Galer, "Un aviso para el Waldorf Astoria," *Poemas*, pp. 128–33.
   Escuchad hambrientos
Advice
   J. Galer, "Consejo," *Poemas*, p. 116.
   "Amigos, les aviso"
Always the Same
   I. Valdés, "Siempre lo mismo," *Antología*, pp. 39–40.
   "En todas partes lo mismo:"
April Rain Song
   J. Galer, "Canción de la lluvia abrileña," *Tiempo Vivo, Revista de Literatura y Arte* nos. 7–8 (July-December 1943), 17. "Deja que"
   Ibid., *Poemas,* p. 71.
Ardella
   Rafael Lozano, "Ardella," *Antología*, p. 36.
   "Te compararía"
   Ibid., *Crisol* 27 (March 1931), p. 230.
   Ibid., *Repertorio Americano* 22 (April 1931), p. 226.
As I Grew Older
   H. Ahumada, "Cuando fui mayor," *Yo también soy,* p. 77.
   "Fue hace mucho tiempo"
   J. Galer, "Cuando fui creciendo," *Poemas*, pp. 30–31.
   "Fue hace mucho, mucho tiempo"
   Concha Zardoya, "Llegada de la vejez," *Alcándara* 1 (1951), p. 10.
   "Era hace mucho tiempo"
   Ibid., *Insula* Nos. 248–49 (1967): 24.
Ballad of Harry Moore
   Manuel González Flores, "La balada de Harry Moore (Asesinado en Mims)," Sunday Supplement to *El Nacional, Revista Mexicana de Cultura* 311 (15 March 1953): 5.
   "Florida—tierra de las flores—"
   Ibid., *Nivel,* 31 (25 July 1961): 4–5.
Ballad of the Landlord
   Manuel González Flores, "La balada del casero," *Poesía de América* 5 (January-February 1953): 77–78.
   "¡Casero! Escucha! Casero!"
   Ibid., *Nivel* 31 (25 July 1961): 4–5.
Beale Street
   J. Galer, "Calle Beale," *Poemas*, p. 76.
   "El sueño es vago"

Birth
> J. Galer, "Alumbramiento," *Poemas,* p. 75.
> "Oh, campos de prodigio"

Blues at Dawn
> H. Ahumada, "Blues de la madrugada," *Yo también,* p. 61.
> "No me atrevo a comenzar la manaña, pensando"

Brass Spitoons
> J. Galer, "Salivaderas de bronce," *Poemas,* pp. 59-60.
> "Limpia las salivaderas, muchacho"

Caribbean Sunset
> J. Galer, "Atardecer caribe," *Poemas,* p. 49.
> "Es que Dios ha tenido una hemorragia"

Chant for May Day
> H. Ahumada, "Canto al día de mayo," *Yo también,* p. 99.
> "Trabajador: El primero de mayo"

Chant for Tom Mooney
> H. Ahumada, "Canto a Tom Mooney, *Yo también,* p. 97.
> "¡Tom Mooney!"

Christ in Alabama
> J. Galer, "Cristo en Alabama," *Poemas,* p. 127.
> "Cristo es un negro"
> Manuel González Flores, "Cristo es un negro," *El Nacional*
> 76 (12 September 1948): 13.
> "Cristo es un negro"

Could Be
> H. Ahumada, "Pudo ser," *Yo también,* p. 71.
> "Pudo ser en la calle Hastings,"

Cross
> Emilio Ballagas, "Mestizaje," *Siempre: Presencia de México*
> 729 (14 June 1967): viii.
> "Un blanco fue mi padre"
> Rafael Lozano, "Cruz," *Crisol* 27 (March 1931): 226.
> "Un blanco fue mi padre"
> Ibid., *Repertorio Americano* 22 (April 1931): 226.
> Ibid., *Antología,* pp. 35-36.
> Mauricio Magdaleno, "Cruz," *La Nueva Democracia* (August 1938): 15.
> "Un blanco fue mi padre"

Dancers
    J. Galer, "Bailarines," *Poemas,* p. 85.
        "Robándole a la noche"
    Ibid., "Bailarines negros," *Poemas,* p. 42.
        "Mi chica y yo"
Danse Africaine
    H. Ahumada, "Danza africana," *Yo también,* p. 35.
        "El quedo batir de los tom-toms"
Daybreak in Alabama
    H. Ahumada, "Aurora en Alabama," *Yo también,* p. 69.
        "Cuando llegue a ser un compositor"
Dear, Lovely Death
    Manuel González Flores, "Amada muerte encantadora," *El Nacional* 76 (12 September 1948): 13.
        "Amada muerte encantadora"
Death
    J. Galer, "Muerte," *Poemas,* p. 86.
        "Dulce, hermosa muerte"
Democracy
    H. Ahumada, "Democracia," *Yo también,* p. 87.
        "La Democracia no llegará"
    J. Galer, "Democracia," *Poemas,* pp. 103–104.
        "La democracia no llegará hoy"
Desire
    J. Galer, "Deseo," *Poemas,* p. 83.
        "El deseo fue a nosotros"
Dream
    J. Galer, "Sueño," *Poemas,* p. 80.
        "Cuando los labios"
Dream Keeper
    H. Ahumada, "El guarda sueños," *Yo también,* p. 13.
        "Traedme todos vuestros sueños"
    J. Galer, "El guarda sueños," *Poemas,* p. 70.
        "Traedme vuestros sueños"
Dreams
    H. Ahumada, "Sueños," *Yo también,* p. 11.
        "Agárrate fuerte a los sueños"
Drum
    J. Galer, "Tambor," *Poemas,* p. 90.
        "Recuerda/que la muerte es un tambor"

Fantasy in Purple
> J. Galer, "Fantasía en púrpura," *Poemas,* p. 48.
> "Suenen los tambores del drama para sí."

Feet O' Jesus
> H. Ahumada, "Pies de Jesús," *Yo también,* p. 41.
> "A los pies de Jesús"

Final Curve
> J. Galer, "Curva final," *Poemas,* p. 110.
> "Cuando al doblar una esquina"

Florida Road Workers
> H. Ahumada, "Trabajadores en un camino de Florida," *Yo también,* p. 89.
> "¡Oye, amigo!"
> Ibid., *Nivel* no. 158 (28 February 1976): 6.
> J. Galer, "Obreros camineros de Florida," *Poemas,* p. 109.
> "Estoy haciendo un camino"

Free Man
> Gastón Figueira, "Puedes agarrar el viento," *La Nueva Democracia* (February 1943): 23.
> "Puedes agarrar el viento"
> Gastón Figueira, "Hombre libre," *Sustancia: Revista de Cultura Superior* (July 1942): 264.
> "Puedes agarrar el viento"

Freedom Train
> J. Galer, "El tren de la libertad," *Orientación* (16 June 1948): 14.
> "He leído en los diarios"
> Ibid., *Poemas,* pp. 121–25.
> Manuel González Flores, "Abordando el tren de la libertad," *Nivel* 31 (25 July 1961): 4–5.
> "Leí en la prensa que el Tren de la Libertad cruza los campos"

Freedom's Plow
> Manuel González Flores, "El arado de la libertad," *América: Tribuna de la Democracia* 52 (October 1946): 63–70.
> "Cuando sin elementos, sin más armas"
> Ibid., *El Nacional* 76 (12 September 1948): 13.
> "¡America!/ Tierra creada en común" (Fragment)

From Selma
> J. Galer, "Desde Selma," *Poemas,* p. 136.
> "En lugares/ Como Selma Alabama"

Genius Child
> H. Ahumada, "Niño pordiosero," *Yo también,* p. 27.
> "¿Qué hay en este niño pordiosero"

Good Morning Revolution
> Miguel Alejandro, "Buenos días, revolución," *Nueva Cultura* (January 1936): 8.
> "¡Buenos días, Revolución!"

Grief
> J. Galer, "Pena," *Poemas,* p. 89.
> "Ojos/ que se hielan"

Harlem
> J. Galer, "Intrigado," *Poemas,* pp. 99–100.
> "Aquí, al borde mismo del infierno"

Harlem Dance Hall
> Tomás Blanco, "Salón de baile en Harlem," *Asomante,* 5 (April-June 1949): 29.
> "Era un salón que estaba sin dignidad"

Harlem Night Club
> H. Ahumada, "Centro nocturno en Harlem," *Yo también,* p. 67.
> "Insinuantes muchachos negros en un cabaret"

Harlem Night Song
> J. Galer, "Canción nocturna de Harlem," *Poemas,* p. 39.
> "Ven"

Hey!
> J. Galer, "¡Hey!," *Poemas,* p. 54.
> "El sol se pone"

Homesick Blues
> J. Galer, "Blues de la añoranza," *Poemas,* pp. 57–58.
> "El puente del ferrocarril"

How About It, Dixie
> H. Ahumada, "Roland Hayes golpeado," *Yo también,* p. 85.
> "Negros"

In Explanation of Our Times
> Anon. "En explicación de nuestros tiempos," *Lunes de Revolución* (n.d.). p. 31.
> "Las gentes sin rótulos delante de sus nombres"

I, Too

H. Ahumada, "Yo también," *Yo también,* p. 79.
"Yo también canto a América"
Ibid., *Nivel,* no. 158 (29 February 1976): 6.
E. Ballagas, "Yo también," *Mapa de la poesía negra americana* (Buenos Aires: Editorial Pleamar, 1946), p. 49.
"Yo también canto América"
Jorge Luis Borges, "Yo también," *Sur* 1 (Fall 1931): 165.
"Yo también canto a América"
José Antonio Fernández de Castro, "Yo, también," *Social* (September 1928): 30.
"Yo también honro a América"
Gastón Figueira, "Yo también," *Aurora* (September 1943): 387–88.
"Yo también canto a América"
Ibid., *Sustancia: Revista de Cultura Superior* (July 1942): 261.
J. Galer, "Yo también," *Poemas,* pp. 52–53.
"Yo también canto, América"
José Luis González, "Yo también," *Siempre, Presencia de México* 729 (14 June 1967): ix.
"Yo también canto a América"
Rafael Lozano, "Yo también," *Antología,* p. 35.
"Yo también canto a América"
Ibid., *Crisol* 27 (March 1931): 227.
Mauricio Magdaleno, "Yo también canto," *La Nueva Democracia* (August 1938): 15.
"Yo también canto a América"
Juan Felipe Toruño, "Yo también," *Poesía negra: Ensayo y antología* (México: Obsidiana, 1953), p. 151.
"Yo también canto a América"
I. Valdés, "Yo también," *Antología,* p. 35.
"Yo también canto a América"
Xavier Villarrutia, "Yo también," *Contemporáneos* 11 (September-October 1931): 157–58.
"Yo también canto a América"
Ibid., *Nivel* 31 (25 July 1961): 4–5.
Jam Session
J. Galer, "Jam Session," *Poemas,* p. 119.
"Dejando a la noche"

Jazz Band in a Parisian Cabaret
>J. Galer, "Jazz Band en un cabaret de París," *Poemas*, pp. 63–64.
>>"Toca esa pieza"

Joy
>H. Ahumada, "Alegría," *Yo también*, p. 55.
>>"Fui a buscar Alegría"
>J. Galer, "Alegría," *Poemas*, p. 40.
>>"Yo fui a buscar la alegría"
>Ibid., *Tiempo Vivo, Revista de Literatura y Arte* nos. 7–8 (July-December 1943): 16.
>Rafael Lozano, "Alegría," *Antología*, p. 38.
>>"Fui en busca de Alegría"
>Ibid., *Crisol* 27 (March 1931): 230–31.
>Ibid., *Repertorio Americano* 22 (April 1931): 226.

Judgment Day
>H. Ahumada, "Juicio final," *Yo también*, p. 51.
>>"Pusieron mi cuerpo en el suelo"

Juke-Box Love Song
>J. Galer, "Canción de amor del Juke Box," *Poemas*, p. 120.
>>"Podría tomar la noche de Harlem"

Justice
>H. Ahumada, "Justicia," *Yo también*, p. 81.
>>"Que la Justicia es una diosa ciega"

Kids Who Die
>H. Ahumada, "Niños que mueren," *Yo también*, p. 109.
>>"Esto es para los niños que mueren,"

Lenox Ave: Midnight
>J. Galer, "Avenida Lenox: Medianoche," *Poemas*, p. 41.
>>"El ritmo de la vida"

Let America Be America Again
>H. Ahumada, "Dejad que América vuelva a ser América," *Yo también*, p. 121.
>>"Dejad que América vuelva a ser América"

Lincoln Monument: Washington
>H. Ahumada, "Monumento de Lincoln: Washington," *Yo también*, p. 63.
>>"Vamos a ver al viejo Abraham"

Little Song
>   J. Galer, "Cancioncilla," *Continente* (15 July 1948): 9.
>   "Gentes solitarias"
>   Ibid., *Poemas*, p. 78.
>   Rafael Lozano, "Cancionera," *Crisol* 27 (March 1931): 227.
>   "Aquella que canta"
>   Ibid., *Repertorio Americano* 22 (April 1931): 226.

Love
>   H. Ahumada, "Amor," *Yo también*, p. 23.
>   "Amor es una alegría violenta"

Man
>   J. Galer, "Hombre," *Continente* (15 July 1948): 9.
>   "Yo era un niño entonces"
>   Ibid., "Hombre," *Poemas*, p. 81.

March Moon
>   J. Galer, "Luna de marzo," *Poemas*, p. 47.
>   "La Luna está desnuda"

Me and the Mule
>   J. Galer, "Yo y mi mula," *Poemas*, p. 95.
>   "Mi vieja mula"

Merry-Go-Round
>   J. Galer, "Carroussel," *Poemas*, p. 94.
>   "Cuál es la sección aparte"
>   José Luis González, "Tíovivo," *Siempre: Presencia de México* 729 (14 June 1967): ix.
>   "¿Dónde está la sección para negros"

Mexican Market Woman
>   Rafael Lozano, "Placera," *Crisol* 27 (March 1931): 227.
>   "Esta pobre vieja"
>   Ibid., *Repertorio Americano* 22 (April 1931): 226.

Minstrel Man
>   H. Ahumada, "Trovador," *Yo también*, p. 15.
>   "Porque mi boca"
>   J. Galer, "El Juglar," *Poemas*, p. 74.
>   "Porque mi boca es llena de risa"

Mother to Son
>   J. Galer, "De madre a hijo," *Poemas*, pp. 34–35.
>   "Y bien, hijo, te diré"

Mulatto

    J. Galer, "Mulato," *Poemas,* pp. 67–69.

    "Soy tu hijo, hombre blanco"

    I. Valdés, "Mulato," *Antología,* pp. 41–43.

    "¡Yo soy su hijo, hombre blanco!"

My People

    H. Ahumada, "Mi gente," *Yo también,* p. 19.

    "La noche es hermosa"

    J. Galer, "Mi pueblo," *Poemas,* p. 36.

    "La noche es bella"

Mystery

    H. Ahumada, "Misterio," *Yo también,* p. 49.

    "Cuando una niña llega a las trece"

Negro

    H. Ahumada, "El negro," *Yo también,* p. 75.

    "Yo soy un negro:"

    E. Ballagas, "Negro," *Mapa de la poesía negra americana* (Buenos Aires: Editorial Pleamar, 1946), pp. 45–47.

    "Soy un negro"

    Eugenio Florit, "El negro," *Antología de la poesía norteamericana contemporánea* (Washington: Union Panamericana, 1955), p. 110.

    "Yo soy un negro"

    J. Galer, "El negro," *Poemas,* pp. 25–26.

    "Soy un negro"

    Rafael Lozano, "Soy un negro," *Antología,* p. 34.

    "Soy un negro"

    Ibid., *Crisol* 27 (March 1931): 228.

    Ibid., *Repertorio Americana* 22 (April 1931): 226.

    Concha Zardoya, "El negro," *Alcándara* 1 (1951): 10.

    "Soy negro,"

    Ibid., *Insula* nos. 248–49 (1967): 24.

Negro Servant

    Tomás Blanco, "Sirviente negro," *Asomante,* 5 (April-June 1949): 31.

    "Todo el día comedido, cortés y bondadoso"

    J. Galer, "Sirviente negro," *Poemas,* pp. 107–108.

    "Todo el día sometido y cortés"

New Moon
   J. Galer, "Luna nueva," *Continente* (15 July 1948): 9.
   "Hay una joven luna nueva"
   Ibid., "Luna nueva," *Poemas*, p. 84.
New Yorkers
   H. Ahumada, "Neoyorquinos," *Yo también*, p. 57.
   "Yo nací aquí,"
Nude Young Dancer
   H. Ahumada, "Joven bailarina desnuda," *Yo también*, p. 37.
   "¿Bajo qué árbol de la jungla has dormido,"
   J. Galer, "Joven bailarina desnuda," *Poemas*, p. 45.
   "Qué árbol de la selva cobijó tú sueño"
One
   J. Galer, "Uno," *Continente* (15 July 1948): 9.
   "Solo,"
   Ibid., "Uno," *Poemas*, p. 77.
One-Way Ticket
   J. Galer, "Boleto de ida sola," *Poemas*, pp. 97–98.
   "Yo tomo mi vida"
Only Woman Blues
   H. Ahumada, "Blues de la mujer única," *Yo también*, p. 65.
   "Quiero hablarte de esa mujer . . . "
Open Letter to the South
   H. Ahumada, "Carta abierta al sur," *Yo también*, p. 105.
   "Trabajadores blancos del Sur:"
Our Land
   H. Ahumada, "Nuestra Tierra," *Yo también*, p. 91.
   "Deberíamos tener una tierra de sol,"
   Jorge Luis Borges, "Nuestra Tierra," *Sur* 1 (Fall 1931): 167.
   "Deberíamos tener una tierra de sol,"
Parisian Beggar Woman
   J. Galer, "Mendiga de París," *Poemas*, p. 72.
   "Fuiste joven una vez"
Park Bench
   H. Ahumada, "Banca del parque," *Yo también*, p. 95.
   "Vivo en una banca del parque . . . "
   J. Galer, "Banco de plaza," *Poemas*, p. 126.
   "Vivo en el banco de una plaza"

Passing
>J. Galer, "Los que pasaron," *Poemas,* p. 118.
>>"En las soleadas domingueras de Harlem"

Passing Love
>H. Ahumada, "Amor pasajero," *Yo también,* p. 33.
>>"Porque eres para mí una canción"
>J. Galer, "Amor pasajero," *Tiempo Vivo, Revista de Literatura y Arte* (July-December 1943): 17.
>>"Porque eres para mí una canción"
>Ibid., *Poemas,* p. 73.

Poem
>H. Ahumada, "A la negra amada," *Yo también,* p. 125.
>>"¡Ah!/mi negra"

Poem
>H. Ahumada, "Poema," *Yo también,* p. 29.
>>"Yo amaba a mi amigo."

Poem (For the portrait of an African boy after the manner of Gauguin)
>E. Ballagas, "Poema," *Mapa de la poesía negra americana* (Buenos Aires: Editorial Pleamar, 1946), p. 53.
>>"Todos los tam-tam de la jungla palpitan en mi sangre,"

Poem
>Xavier Villarrutia, "Poema," *Contemporáneos* 11 (September-October 1931): 158.
>>"La noche es bella,"

Port Town
>Rafael Lozano, "Puerto," *Antología,* p. 37.
>>"¡Hola!, Marinero"
>Ibid., *Crisol* 27 (March 1931): 230.
>Ibid., *Repertorio Americano* 22 (April 1931): 226.

Porter
>J. Galer "Sirviente," *Poemas,* p. 65.
>>"Debo decirte, Yes Sir"

Po' Boy Blues
>H. Ahumada, "Blues del pobrecito," *Yo también,* p. 17.
>>"Cuando estaba en casa"
>Gastón Figueira, "Blues del pobre muchacho," *Aurora* (September 1953): 387–88.
>>"Cuando yo estaba en mi casa"

Ibid., *Sustancia: Revista de Cultura Superior* (July 1942): 262.

J. Galer, "Blues del pobre muchacho," *Poemas,* pp. 55–56.

"Cuando yo estaba en mi casa"

Prayer

H. Ahumada, "Oración," *Yo también,* p. 43.

"Te pregunto esto:"

J. Galer, "Oración," *Poemas,* p. 66.

"Yo te pregunto Dios"

Xavier Villarrutia, "Plegaria," *Contemporáneos* 11 (September-October 1931): 158.

"Yo te pregunto"

Prelude from Weary Blues

Emilio Ballagas, "Preludio a 'Weary Blues'," *Mapa de la poesía negra americana* (Buenos Aires: Editorial Pleamar, 1946), pp. 45–47.

"Soy un negro" [Same as "Negro"]

Pride

H. Ahumada, "Orgullo," *Yo también,* p. 93.

"Dejad que todos los que quieran,"

Question

J. Galer, "Pregunta," *Poemas,* p. 88.

"Cuando ese viejo recolector de chatarra"

Quiet Girl

H. Ahumada, "Niña silenciosa," *Yo también,* p. 21.

"Diría que eres"

Reverie on the Harlem River

Gastón Figueira, "No fuiste nunca junto al río," *La Nueva Democracia* (February 1943): 23.

"No fuiste nunca junto al río,"

Ibid., "Reverie en el río Harlem," *Sustancia: Revista de Cultura Superior* (July 1942): 264.

Roar China

Lino Novás Calvo, "Ruge China," *Ayuda* (18 September 1937): 1.

"¡Ruge China"

Ibid., *Repertorio Americano* 34 (6 November 1937): 260.

Ruby Brown
    J. Galer, "Ruby Brown," *Poemas,* pp. 61–62.
    "Era joven y hermosa"
Share Croppers
    J. Galer, "Peones," *Poemas,* p. 96.
    "Sólo un rebaño de negros"
Silence
    J. Galer, "Silencio," *Poemas,* p. 79.
    "Yo siento el modo/de tu silencio"
Sister Johnson Marches
    H. Ahumada, "La hermana Johnson marcha," *Yo también,*
    p. 119.
    "¡Aquí estoy yo con la cabeza bien alta!"
Six-Bits Blues
    J. Galer, "Un peso de Blues," *Poemas,* p. 93.
    "Déme un peso de boleto"
Slave Song
    J. Galer, "Canción del esclavo," *Poemas,* p. 134.
    "Puedo ver a lo lejos"
Sliver of Sermon
    H. Ahumada, "Plata de sermón," *Yo también,* p. 47.
    "Cuando los alcahuetes desde la soledad claman:"
Soledad
    J. Galer, "Soledad (Un retrato cubano)," *Poemas,* p. 50.
    "Las sombras"
    Rafael Lozano, "Soledad," *Crisol* 27 (March 1931): 226–27.
    "Las sombras"
    Ibid., *Repertorio Americano* 22 (April 1931): 226.
Song
    H. Ahumada, "Canción," *Yo también,* p. 31.
    "Amada obscura y solitaria . . . "
Song for a Dark Girl
    E. Ballagas, "Canto de una joven negra," *Mapa de la poesía
negra americana* (Buenos Aires: Editorial Pleamar, 1946), p.
51.
    "Fue allá en el Sur, en el Sur."
    G. Caprario, "Canto de una muchacha negra," *Antología,* p.
38.
    "Allá lejos, en el sur,"

Gastón Figueira, "Canción de una muchacha negra," *Aurora* (September 1943): 387–88.

"Allá, al sur, lejos, en Dixie,"

Ibid., *Sustancia: Revista de Cultura Superior* (July 1942): 263.

Silvestre Revueltas, "Canto de una muchacha negra," *Contemporary Latin American Composers* (New York: E. B. Marks Music Corp., 1948) No pagination. Note reads: "Revueltas wrote the music of this translation [presumably his own] of Langston Hughes's poem."

"Allá lejos en el Sur"

Song of Spain

H. Ahumada, "El canto de España," *Yo también*, p. 101.

"Vengan ahora todos los cancioneros,"

Ibid., *Nivel*, no. 158 (28 February 1976): 6.

Song to a Negro Wash Woman

J. Galer, "Canto a una lavandera negra," *Poemas*, pp. 137–39.

"Oh, lavandera"

Songs

J. Galer, "Canciones," *Poemas*, p. 82.

"Yo, a su lado, le cantaba"

Stalingrad: 1942

J. Galer, "Stalingrad: 1942," *Poemas*, pp. 140–45.

"Están los inactivos"

Stars

Ariel Canzani, "Oh, amor de estrellas sobre la calle de Harlem," *Revista Internacional de poesía* (October 1963): 1.

"Oh, amor de estrellas sobre la calle de Harlem,"

Tomás Blanco, "Estrellas," *Asomante* 5 (April-June 1949): 29.

"¡Oh, roció de estrellas en el cielo de Harlem!"

Suicide's Note

J. Galer, "La nota del suicidio," *Poemas*, p. 46.

"El calmo"

Xavier Villaurrutia, "Nota de un suicidio," *Contemporáneos*, 11 (September-October 1931): 159.

"La serena"

Subway Rush Hour
    J. Galer, "Mediodía en el subte," *Poemas,* p. 117.
        "Mezclados/Aliento y sudor"
Sunday
    Eugenio Florit, "Domingo," *Antología de la poesía nor-
teamericana contemporánea* (Washington: *Union Pan-
americana,* 1955), p. 112.
        "No me he vestido en todo el día"
Sunday Morning Prophecy
    J. Galer, "Profecía del domingo a la mañana," *Poemas,* pp.
111-13.
        "Habiendo previamente señalado los pecados"
Tell Me
    J. Galer, "Dime," *Poemas,* p. 114.
        "Por qué ha de ser mi soledad"
Testament
    H. Ahumada, "Testimonio," *Yo también,* p. 45.
        "Si tan sólo tuviera un piano . . . "
The Cat and the Saxophone: 2 a.m.
    J. Galer, "El gato y el saxofón (Dos de la mañana)", *Poemas,*
pp. 43-44.
        "Todos quieren"
The Jester,
    J. Galer, "El bufón," *Poemas,* p. 37.
        "Llevo en una mano la tragedia"
The Negro Speaks of Rivers
    Jorge Luis Borges, "El negro habla de los ríos," *Sur* 1 (Fall
1931): 169.
        "He conocido ríos"
    J. Galer, "El negro habla de los ríos," *Poemas,* p. 29.
        "Yo he conocido ríos viejos como el mundo, y"
    Rafael Lozano, "El negro habla de los ríos," *Antología,* pp.
36-37.
        "Conozco algunos ríos"
    Ibid., *Crisol* 27 (March 1931): 229.
    Ibid., *Repertorio Americano* 22 (April 1931): 226.
    Xavier Villarrutia, "El negro habla de los ríos," *Nivel* 31 (25
July 1961): 4-5.
        "He conocido ríos"

Ibid., *Siempre: Presencia de México* 729 (14 June 1967): viii.
The South
    J. Galer, "El Sur," *Poemas,* pp. 32–33.
       "El languido, riente Sur"
The Weary Blues
    J. Galer, "Los blues tristes,".*Poemas,* pp. 27–28.
       "Tararareando una soñolienta, sincopada, melodía"
Union
    H. Ahumada, "Unión," *Yo también,* p. 117.
       "Yo solo no:"
    I. Valdés, "Unión," *Antología,* p. 41.
       "No quiero estar solo . . . "
Vagabonds
    J. Galer, "Vagabundos," *Poemas,* p. 87.
       "Somos los desesperados"
Visitors to the Black Belt
    J. Galer, "Visitantes en el barrio negro," *Poemas,* pp. 101–102.
       "Ustedes pueden decir"
When Sue Wears Red
    H. Ahumada, "Cuando Susana se viste de rojo," *Yo también,* p. 53.
       "Cuando Susana Jones se viste de rojo"
    J. Galer, "Cuando Susana Jones se viste de rojo," *Poemas,* p. 38.
       "Cuando Susana Jones se viste de rojo"
Who But the Lord
    H. Ahumada, "¿Quién, si no el Señor?" *Yo también,* p. 83.
       "Miré y vi"
    J. Galer, "Quién sino el Señor," *Poemas,* pp. 105–106.
       "Alcé mis ojos y vi"
Winter Sweetness
    H. Ahumada, "Dulzura invernal," *Yo también,* p. 25.
       "Esta casita es de azúcar . . . "
Wonderful World
    Anon. "Mundo de prodigios," *Bayoan*
       "Lecho maravilloso"

[Hughes wrote the following in "Ten Ways to Use Poetry in Teaching," *CLA Journal,* 11 (June 1968): 278: "Here is a recent Puerto Rican translation of a poem of my own as published in *Bayoan.*" No translator was given and I have not seen this item (E.J.M.)]

Yesterday and Today

    H. Ahumada, "Ayer y hoy," *Yo también,* p. 73.

    "Oh, desearía que ayer"

Youth

    H. Ahumada, "Juventud," *Yo también,* p. 39.

    "Tenemos el manaña"

    J. Galer, "Juventud," *Poemas,* p. 51.

    "Tenemos el mañana"

I. PROSE

Mexico

MEXICAN GAMES

Lady White

One child is chosen as Lady White and another as Don Philip, her suitor. All the other players join hands to form a large circle, thus making a house for Lady White, who stands in the center. Don Philip comes to call and begins to walk around the circle, but finds every hand tightly joined and so he can not get in. The children forming the ring then sing the following verse three times:

> Sweet Lady White is sheltered
> In walls of silver and gold;
> Her lover must break a window,
> The Lady to behold.

Then Lady White asks:
> Who is walking around my house?

And the lover answers:
> Don Philip Philipon.

And the Lady says:
> Why, who can this fat person be?

And the suitor replies:
> Don Philip Philipon.

Then the players in the circle all sing:
> You can't get into this house,
> Don Philip Philipon;
> Unless you break a window out.
> Don Philip Philipon.

Then Don Philip attempts to break through the circle in order to reach the inside. As soon as he succeeds in getting in, however, Lady White must run out and Don Philip has to catch her. Then the game may be played over again with two different children taking the parts of Don Philip and Lady White.

The Lost Donkey

Here is a game to be played when there is an odd number of children present so that when pairs are formed there will always be one left over. All the players walk about in different directions and pretend to be gathering flowers while they sing this little song:

> Benny goes a walking,
> Picking pretty flowers.
> Benny goes a walking
> Under shady bowers.
> But he shall lose his way,
> Little donkey,
> And be alone all day,
> Little donkey.
> And be alone all day,
> Little donkey.

At the third *Little Donkey* all the players must run to join hands with another player so as to have a partner and the one who is left without a partner is the *Little Lost Donkey* until the next game gives him a chance to get one.

The Priest and the Teacher

In this game one child is a priest, another is a teacher and the third a storekeeper. The priest and the teacher are buyers. All the other children are articles of merchandise and should sit down in a long line. To each one in line the storekeeper gives a secret name such as *Butter, Sugar, Cinnamon,* and so on, which the buyers must not know. Then the priest and the teacher take turns at buying and can only ask for one article at a time. For example, if the priest calls for

Cheese, the player who has that name must rise and follow him, but if there is no *cheese* the storekeeper says so and the priest must wait until his next turn to ask for something else. When the storekeeper has sold all his merchandise the priest and the teacher count their articles and the one who has the most can be storekeeper for the next time, and he also has the privilege of choosing the new priest and the new teacher.

Dear Little Friends:

These are three games which the children play in your beautiful neighbor country, Mexico. I hope you will enjoy them.

From: *The Brownies Book*, January 1921, p. 18.

IN A MEXICAN CITY

Toluca sits in the highest plateau of Mexico at the foot of the old and long extinct volcano "Xinantecatl," which is said to be named after one of the ancient Indian kings. All around us there are mountains and our valley is broad and fertile. Here the climate is cool and often cold, but the poor folks never have shoes to wear nor do the rich use stoves in their houses. In summer it is the rainy season and every day brings long showers and misty clouds that hide the mountains. In winter the sky is clear and the sun shines warm at mid-day, but in the shade it is always cool.

The house where I live faces a little plaza or park and from my window I can see many interesting things. Every morning a bare-footed old woman in a wide straw hat and long skirts drives a little flock of white sheep down the street, and sometimes she has a tiny baby lamb in her arms. They go to the country to graze all day and in the evening they come back again. Often I see a funeral procession passing through the plaza on the way to the Panteon and as they do not have hearses here, the men carry the casket on their shoulders while the mourners walk behind them. On Sundays the park is full of black-shawled women and men wrapped in *serapes* or blankets who come in the early morning to say mass in the quaint old church in front with its pretty tower and its most unmusical bells.

There are many churches here and all of them are very old. Some were built before the Independence, when Mexico was still under Spanish rule, and have beautiful domes and tall, graceful towers. Practically every one is Catholic and they keep many feast days. On the day of the Innocent Saints there is a custom that reminds one of our April Fool. On this date things should never be loaned and if you forget, the article is sure to be sent back by the joking friend who borrowed it, accompanied by a tiny box full of tiny toys and a note calling you a "poor little innocent saint." On the second of November, which is a day in honor of the dead, they sell many little cardboard coffins and paper dolls dressed as mourners, and if a person meets you in the street and says "I'm dying" first; then, of course, he has to treat you to the present. On a certain day in January the people take their animals to be blessed and in the church-yard one sees everything from oxen to rabbits. Each is wearing a bit of gay colored ribbon and they wait patiently for the priest to come.

The houses here from the outside all look very much alike and are but a succession of arched doors and windows with small balconies facing the sidewalk. They often have lovely court-yards and verandas but these are hidden from the passers-by behind high walls, and the fronts of the houses never tell anything about the beauty that may be within them. When one enters a house the door usually leads directly into the court-yard or sometimes into the long open corridor from which every room has its entrance. In the *patio* or court-yard there are flowers the year round and if it is a large one, there may be a garden or trees. On the railing of the long veranda, too, there are many pots of red and pink geraniums and fragrant heliotrope. Inside the house there will probably be little furniture. Only a few of the well-to-do people have a great deal, so most of the homes use chairs as their principal space fillers. In a friend's parlor I counted twenty-seven one day and the only other articles of furniture were two small tables. Most of the parlors of the middle-class folk show the same emptiness but perhaps it is a good idea, for on holidays there is plenty of room to dance without moving anything out.

The kitchens here are very different from American ones, for they do not use stoves or gas ranges. The fuel is charcoal and the stoves are made of stone or brick, built into the wall like a long seat, except that they have three square grates on top for the fire and three square holes in front for removing the ashes. Some are prettily built and covered with gaily colored tiles. To make the fire several splinters of pine are lighted in the grate and then the black pieces of charcoal piled on top. Then one must fan and fan at the square holes in front until the charcoal on top begins to blaze, and in a little while you have a nice glowing fire ready to cook with.

The shops here in the portals, which is Toluca's "uptown," are much like the American stores, but in the little *expendios* in the side streets one can buy a penny's worth of wood or a tablespoonful of lard or a lamp full of oil. The poor here do not have much money. These little shops paint themselves all sorts of colors and have the funniest names. One I know is called "The Wedding Bouquet." Others are "The Light of America," "The Big Fight," "The Fox," and so on, and one tinner's shop is even called "Heart of Jesus." The last store on the edge of town, where the road leads off to San Juan, has the very appropriate name of "Farewell." One who did know Spanish could acquire a whole vocabulary just by reading the store names which are painted in large colored letters across the front and are often accompanied by pictures or decorations to illustrate their meanings. For instance, the meat market called "The Bull of Atenco" has the animal's picture on one side of the door and a bull-fighter's on the other, painted over a background of bright blue.

Friday is market-day in Toluca and the square outside the market-house is one sea of wide Mexican hats, as buyer and trader jostle and bargain. The surrounding streets are lined with Indians from the country who squat behind their little piles of vegetables, or fruit, or herbs, which they have to sell and which they spread out on the ground before them. One old woman will have neat little piles of green peppers for a cent a pile. Another will have beans and another wild herbs for seasoning soup or making medicine. The fruit sellers, of course, always have a most gorgeous and luscious display. Under a canopy created from four sticks and some sort of covering to make a spot of shade, are piled all sorts of strange, delicious fruits. There one finds creamy alligator pears and queer-tasting mangoes; red pomegranates and black zapotes; small, round melons and fat little bananas and the delicately flavored granada, which feels like a paper ball and has a soft seedy pulp inside. Then there are oranges that come up to us from the hot country, along with limes and juicy lemons that are not sour like the ones we know up north.

Here people never buy without bargaining. If the price asked for a thing is two cents, they are sure to get it for one. The price arguments are always good-natured and the merchant, knowing that he will have to come down, usually asks more than he should in the first place. Everyone going to market must carry his own baskets and sacks and even the paper for his meat, as everything is sold without wrapping.

A market-day crowd is composed of all sorts of people. A rich señorita with her black scarf draped gracefully about her shoulders is doing the family buying, while the servants carrying baskets follow behind. Indian women with sacks of vegetables on their backs; others with turkeys or chickens in their arms; little ragged brown boys seeking a chance to earn a few cents by carrying a customer's basket; and beggars, numberless beggars, blind, lame and sick beggars, all asking patiently for pennies or half rotted fruits; these are the folks one sees on market-day pushing and elbowing their way through the crowd which is so thick that nobody can hurry.

On one side of the plaza are the sellers of hats and the large yellow mats that the Indians spread down on the floor at night for sleeping purposes. The Mexican straw hats have wide round brims and high peaked crowns and, though cheap, most of them are prettily shaped. The Indian, upon buying a new hat, will not take the trouble to remove his old one, but puts the new one on top and marches off home with his double decked head gear. Sometimes a hat merchant, desiring to change his location, will put one hat on his head, and as each peaked crown fits snugly over the other, he then piles his whole stock on top of himself and goes walking down the street like a Chinese pagoda out for a stroll.

Here everything that people do not carry on their backs they carry on their heads. The ice-cream man crying *nieve*, balances his freezer, and the baker-boys carrying a shallow basket as big around as a wagon wheel. This basket has a crown in the center and when filled with bread it fits over the head like a very wide Mexican hat, while its wearer underneath is as insignificant as the stem of a mushroom. Sometimes we see fruit sellers, too, with great colorful mounds of fruit piled upon their wooden trays and balanced gracefully on their black-haired heads. When a thing is too heavy or too unwieldy to put on the head, then it is carried on the back, and the Indians bear immense burdens in this way. Men, women and even small children are often seen with great loads of wood or charcoal, or sacks of grain, on their backs and the only carriage that the little Indian baby ever knows is its mother's back, where it rides contented all day long, tied in her *rebosa* or shawl.

From *The Brownies Book*, April 1921, pp. 102–105.

THE VIRGIN OF GUADALUPE

After the coming of the Spaniards, who brought priests and missionaries, as well as soldiers to conquer Mexico, most of the subdued Indians were converted to the faith of the Catholics. The ancient Indian temples to barbaric gods were torn down by the Europeans who built new Christian churches in their stead. Thus it came about that the brown men learned to worship the saints and idols brought by the invaders and so forgot their old gods.

One day a pious follower of the Spaniards' faith, Juan Diego by name, was returning from mass across the hill of Guadalupe, when suddenly a veiled figure, all light and beauty, appeared before him. The poor Indian was much astonished and filled with surprise when the woman spoke to him and commanded in a soft voice that he go to the bishop and tell His Excellency to construct a church on the hill where the figure was standing. This Juan did, or attempted to do, but the bishop's servants, thinking the man a common ignorant Indian, would not give him admission to the house, so Juan Diego went back.

For a second time the vision appeared before him, issuing the same command in her beautiful voice, so the Indian returned in search of the bishop. Each time, however, he was refused an entry but the vision told him to persevere. Finally, after many days, he was admitted and the old father asked him what he wished. When Juan Diego told of the beautiful spirit and her message, the bishop could not believe such a tale and thought perhaps that the poor fellow was demented. At last he told the Indian that he would have to bring some sign or token of proof in support of his strange words.

Once more the man returned to the hill and there at its foot the bright vision reappeared. Hearing the message that the bishop had sent, she said, "Pluck those flowers there at your feet." But Juan Diego, standing on the bare and rocky earth, asked, "What flowers?" Then suddenly looking down he saw the ground covered with white blossoms which he began to pick and with which he filled his small woven *tilma* or mantle, used to wrap about his shoulders on cold mornings.

Then he went to the bishop and said, "Here is your sign." Opening the mantle the white flowers rolled out at their feet. The bishop looked, but still more marvellous than the flowers, the surprised priest saw, painted on the mantle where the blossoms had been the figure of the Virgin surrounded by a halo of light. "This," he said, "is surely the proof." So they proceeded to erect the church on the top of the hill. Later a magnificent cathedral was built at its foot where the *tilma* bearing the picture of the Virgin is preserved to this day above the altar and on the spot where the vision first appeared, a spring of water gushed forth and is now covered by a pretty shrine where people may stop to drink.

Once a year a great *fiesta* is held in honor of this patron saint of Mexico and many people come from far away to visit her. Any day when one cares to take a trip out to the stately church where she is housed near Mexico City, her faithful worshippers may be seen going on their knees the long distance from the outside door to the high altar carrying white candles in their hands, crawling up to place them before her—La Virgin de Guadalupe—whose name is known and loved by all Mexico.

From: *The Crisis,* 23 (December 1921): 77.

UP TO THE CRATER OF AN OLD VOLCANO

Near Toluca, Mexico, is an old volcano, Xinantecatl. The fires which once burned within its bosom have long ago gone out and now, in the deep crater that in past centuries held boiling lava and red hot ashes, two calm blue lakes sparkle like dainty jewels in a rough setting. No one knows when the last eruption of this volcano took place but some say that it was long before the time of Christ, and when the Aztec Indians came down from the North to found their powerful empire, Xinantecatl, for so they called it, had long been sleeping. Now, like a dead giant at rest, it is still great and majestic. Rising above the puny cities and little low hills that cluster about its base, it is as some nature king rising above a subject people. The ancient Indians thought it a god and climbed its steep sides carrying gold and jewels and precious gifts on their backs as an offering to the mountain deity. Even today the rural Indians say that when shots are fired in the crater or stones thrown into the blue lakes, the mountain becomes angry and calls the clouds to hide its peaks and send rain down upon its disturbers. We in Toluca, however, are not afraid of Xinantecatl. It is like a well known friend to us and one whom we see every day. On clear mornings its peaks are sharp and distinct in the blue sky; at evening the whole mountain makes a great black silhouette against the twilight colors.

When the boys of the Instituto, Toluca's high school, began to plan a two-day walking trip to the crater, and invited me to go with them, I accepted eagerly. They, with the customary Mexican politeness, put my name first on the list of those who were to go and several of the students went with me to aid in choosing the proper kind of "trumpeate," a sort of bag for carrying food. It is woven from marsh grass and is light of weight. They also saw that I bought a wide Mexican hat, as protection from the sun, and told me all the things that I would need to carry. First, plenty of lunch; then, two warm blankets because we were to sleep in the open mountains; my camera for pictures; a bottle for water; a small amount of cognac or some other liquor in case of mountain sickness in the high altitude; and a pistol. "But above all," they said, "take onions!" Those who had been up to the volcano before claimed that they were the very best things to smell if one began to feel ill in the thin air near the summit. I thought to myself that if I should get sick, the scent of onions would only make me worse. Nevertheless I took them and when the time arrived for their use I found my mind completely changed about their smell.

It was a beautiful sunny morning when we left Toluca. From the platform of the small station, where we were to board the seven o'clock train for Calimaya, we could see the white, sparkling snow peaks of the volcano and they seemed very high and far away. There were forty of us going on the trip and, before leaving time, the first coach of the tiny train was completely filled with Instituto boys. The aisle of the car was one jumble of blanket rolls and fat "trumpeates" of food, and the windows were crowded with faces—mostly brown faces of laughing young fellows, all talking at once and watching the late comers hurrying down the platform. These dark faced, friendly school boys were about like other dark skinned boys of my own race whom I had known in the United States. They made me remember a hike that the colored Y.M.C.A. fellows, in Chicago, took out to the sand dunes one summer. There the car windows were crowded with dark faces, too, and everybody talked at once. The only difference was that in Chicago they were speaking English and when a late member of the party reached the platform, every one cried out, "Hurry up!" while here, when Rudolfo, the tardy, came running through the gates, every one in the window shouted, "Apurese!" which means the same in Spanish.

The little train went click, click, click, down the pretty valley. We passed several small villages: Metepec, with its great church large enough to hold its whole population; San Francisco, a collection of small huts, and a white temple; Mexicaltzingo, where the country bull-fights are held; and then Calimaya, where the road to the volcano begins.

We found Calimaya a small, clean town with cobblestone streets and a stream of water running down the center of each one, where the cows and long horned oxen stopped to drink.

We piled our blankets and bags in one corner of its arched "Portales" to wait while two of the boys went for the guide and the burros—patient little beasts of burden—who were to carry our things. After a long while the burros came. There had been some disagreement in regard to the money to be paid, so we learned, the guide having set a price and then suddenly changing his mind, saying that he could not risk his animals in the cold mountain air for such a small sum. But finally an agreement was reached and we had three burros, a boy and two men to drive them, and a guide—all for a price that would amount to but five American dollars, and this for a two-day trip!

When the word "Vamanos" was given, the three small animals were almost hidden under their loads of blankets and lunch-bags, but being strong, sturdy little beasts, they did not seem to mind. They started off down the road with a trot, the two drivers and the boy running behind shouting, "Burro! Burro!" to make them go faster. The members of the hiking party, freed of their luggage, had nothing to pack now except the canteens or water bottles and their guns. Very few having pistols, there was an unusual variety of fire-arms in sight, from a modern rifle to ancient carbines. The reason for so many shooting machines was that we might meet bandits on the road, and, though it was only a *might,* every one should be prepared. During the revolutions and until a year or so ago the hills were full of robbers, who, not content with taking travelers' money, would ofttimes take their clothes, even to their shoes, leaving the robbed ones to get home as best they could. Now, though such robberies are infrequent, no one goes far into the country unarmed. The boys of the Instituto, going through the quaint streets of Calimaya, looked like a small militia.

The road leading to the foothills was quite bare of trees. High in a cloudless sky, the sun beat down upon our heads without pity, while the dust rose in clouds from under our feet. On either side the road was lined with maguey and cactus plants which served as a sort of fence around the fields, where lazy, slow moving oxen were pulling wooden plows yoked to their horns, and wide-hatted peons pricked them languidly with sharp-pointed sticks. After about an hour's walking we passed Zaragoza, a small village which, like all Mexican villages, had its tall old church towering sad and beautiful above the miserable little huts. By this time all our water bottles were empty and our throats were dry. The guide promised us that we should come to a river soon and when we finally reached its friendly banks, after what seemed like an eternity of tramping in dust and sun, we lay on our stomachs like dogs and drank the cool clear water that came rippling down from the hills.

Soon the road began to ascend and we found ourselves climbing a slope covered with little pine trees. Before us, when we reached the summit, we saw only pine clad hills and then more hills, hiding the volcano from us. Looking back, we saw the wide valley of Toluca below, dotted with red roofed villages and the white towers and domes of old, old churches. At its opposite side we saw the mountains rising like a wall about the valley, shutting it in from the rest of the world and protecting it with their grey and purple strength.

The road now led upward, and it was not easy climbing through the forest of stunted trees with the sun like a hot ball overhead. About one o'clock, when everybody was aching and tired, the guide showed us a little cañon at one side of the road and said that here was the last water to be found before reaching the crater, the next morning; so he advised us to stop for lunch and to fill our water bottles. The burros were unloaded and everyone searched in the pile of "trumpeates" for his lunch-bag. As each woven sack looked just about like another, there was much opening and exchanging and inspecting before each one had his own. Then we scattered about the slope and prepared to eat. One of the boys from each group went down to the spring for water, and it was deliciously sweet and cool. After lunch we decided to rest a while. The guide said we had made good time and in three hours we could reach the timber line, where we were to make camp on the edge of the woods.

At three o'clock we climbed up to the road, loaded the burros and were off again—up, up, up. We had left the foot-hills behind us now and were on the very slope of the volcano itself. Here the trees, taller and thicker, made what we call a real forest. Perhaps we had eaten too much lunch, or perhaps we were tired, but anyway the trail seemed difficult. Then, too, we had begun to notice the lightness of the air and at every hundred yards or so we had to stop for breath. Some of the boys began to feel ill and at this juncture the onions put in their appearance. I felt none too well, so I began to search in my pockets for my onions, too,—and when, with a dull ache in my head and a breathless feeling in the lungs, I pressed them to my nose, all the former aversion to their scent disappeared. I kept them under my nose all the way to camp. And whether due to the onions or not, I didn't feel any worse while some of the fellows had to walk so slowly that they were left behind the rest of the party.

In the late afternoon we passed through a part of the forest where it seemed as if more than half the trees had been torn up by the roots.

Great tree trunks, so large that we could hardly climb over them, lay across the path. Looking down, I could see whole hillsides strewn with these fallen members of the forest. Some of the boys explained to me how, two years before, a hurricane had swept across the mountains and tried to carry the whole forest off with it. The fallen trees were a bad impediment to our progress because, in an atmosphere where one cannot walk without getting out of breath, to climb over a gigantic trunk is an exercise that is not taken with pleasure.

It was almost six o'clock when we arrived at the spot chosen for camp, just below the timber line, where the trees of the mountain end. We were close to the peaks now and one of them, that looked very near, loomed between us and the sinking sun so that all the mountain-side was in shadow. Down below we saw the valley—far, far beneath—bathed in a twilight mist of rose and purple; the little river, that had been a winding, silver thread all day, had now turned golden in the sunset.

We began to make camp. Some unloaded the burros and tied them fast to trees. Others searched for the dry limbs and branches of the pine in order to make the fires. And still others, too tired and out of breath to do anything, sank down upon the ground to rest, for the last hour of the ascent had been the hardest of all.

The shadows on the mountain-side deepened and the sunset colors faded from the sky. For me, the evening passed quickly. There was supper around the blazing camp-fires, of which each group of fellows had its own; then songs and stories and more songs, to which the two burro drivers contributed a love ballad which they said they had learned down in the "hot country." At nine, the first guards were posted and the camp became still. The only noise to be heard was the occasional sob-like "hee-hooing" of the burros and the strong "Alerta" of the watchers, crying to each other from the four corners of the camp.

At two o'clock, when my turn came to stand guard, the moon had gone down behind the mountain and the forest was in inky blackness. The low burning camp-fires gave a little light. A long way off and deep down in the night-covered valley, we saw the white lights of Toluca, shining like a cluster of sunken stars in the darkness.

The next morning, at sunrise, we were off for the crater. A half hour's walk took us past the timber line, out of the forest, and to the open mountain-side. In a little while we found ourselves at the foot of one of the volcanic peaks, which, if we chose to climb it, would give us a view down into the crater. About half the party chose to go up; the others took the burro path which led around the side of the peak, entering the crater at the lowest opening. The peak, which near the top was covered with large patches of snow, did not appear to be very high. But we soon found that the steepness of its slope and the lightness of the air made the ascent more laborious than we thought it would be, and at every eight or ten steps we had to stop for breath. It seemed as if we would never reach the summit. The rocks and sand and gravel, of which the mountain was made, slipped beneath our feet and made us slide half-way back at every forward movement. We had to cross the snow covered spaces on our hands and knees—they were so slippery. When we finally gained the summit, it seemed as if our last breath had gone. We were very high and, between us and the hills below, the white clouds drifted by. As we turned to look down into the crater, we saw it as a sort of double one, divided into two parts by a long hump-backed hill. On each side of the hill there was a blue lake with a rocky shore. The sides of the crater were steep and many colored, and the three highest of the tall, jagged peaks that formed its ragged edge had snow upon them. We, on top of our laboriously climbed summit, had an excellent view down into that part of the volcano where La Laguna Chica (The Little Lake) sparkled in the morning sun. Those who had taken the burro path were already resting on its shore and the height from which we saw them made them appear very tiny. Feeling the pangs of hunger, as we had not yet eaten breakfast, and knowing that the burros carrying the lunch-bags were waiting for us below, we began to descend. Half running, half sliding in the loose sand and gravel of the inner slope, we reached the bottom much more quickly than we had ascended. On the sandy shore, scattered with big boulders taller than a man, we ate our breakfast and drank the cold, refreshing water of the clear blue lake.

After breakfast we decided to see La Laguna Grande (The Big Lake), and so, circling around the side of The Little Lake, we began to climb one of the low ends of the hump-backed hill. In a short while, from the top of its rocky ridge, we saw below us the deep blue waters of La Laguna Grande, so beautiful and lovely and calm that it gave one a thrill of surprise at finding it buried in this old volcano's burnt, scarred walls. Some people say that this pretty lake has no bottom and that swimmers who venture far into its cold waters may be drawn down into unknown depths. Its smooth, innocent surface, however, gives no indications of such treachery, and the charm of its beauty makes one think it is a good fairy lake and not the wicked old witch with the pretty face, which reputation has given it.

We walked all around the rocky shore, stopping now and then to pick up small queer-colored stones or the sulphur coated rocks found on the beach. To reach the other end of the lake's long oval required more time than we had expected, for distances are deceiving in the high clear air. We stopped often to rest, sitting down on the large boulders and admiring the beautiful colors in the sides of the crater whose walls were sometimes deep crimson capped with jagged peaks, sometimes bright red or soft orange streaked with purple, and sometimes just gray rock covered with snow patches near the rim. And the blue lake was always like a jewel in a rough setting. At the other end of the oval we found erected on the sandy shore, a large wooden cross which a band of religious people had carried up the steep trail some years before. They held a mass in the crater. Behind the cross rose "El Pice de Fraile," the highest of the Xinantecatl peaks, glittering snow white in morning sun. From its tooth-like summit on a clear day, one who has a pair of strong binoculars can see, off the coast of Guerrero, more than a hundred miles away, the silver waters of the Pacific.

When we climbed back over the hump-backed hill and down to the wider shore of the Little Lake, the burros were already packed with our blankets and much diminished lunch-bags. Before we reached the spot where we had eaten, the first ones started off. We filled our water bottles and canteens from the lake and started after them. When we came to the highest point in the narrow road we turned for a last look at the little blue lake below, the hump-backed hill and the opposite red and purple walls of the volcano. Then we turned and followed the path which curved, at a dizzying height, onto the steeply sloping outer sides of the crater, when a false step too near the edge would have sent one tumbling down a mile or so into a green tree-covered valley. We took care not to make the false step.

When, at sunset, we unloaded the burros in the clean little "Portales" of Calimaya, although stiff and footsore and weary, everybody was happy and agreed that it had been a fine trip. A few minutes later, sitting on the platform of the country station, awaiting the last train for Toluca, we could see, high and far away, the sharp, jagged peaks of the old volcano faintly outlined against the sunset sky. They seemed so very high and so very far from us we could scarcely believe that just ten hours before we had visited them and drunk the cool snow water of their clear blue lakes.

From: *The Brownies Book,* December 1921, pp. 334-38.

LOVE IN MEXICO

Pictures of yesterday down a long telescope of bittersweet memories: I was nineteen when I went to live in Mexico with my father. I knew very little Spanish then, but I began to learn and gradually I was able to talk with the people and to know them.

In Toluca, high mountain town where my father lived, the evening promenade was an established institution for young folks of the town, and on band concert nights, for the older people, too. Toluca's small, concentrated, run-down business district consisted largely of three sides of a square with a cloistered walk running around the three sides. (An enormous and very old church formed the fourth side of the square.) This covered walkway had tall arched portals open to the cobblestoned street, hence its name, *Los Portales.*

The leading shops were along the *Portales.* The Post Office was there as well. And the biggest hotel. And a very appetizing chocolate and sweet shop displaying enormous layer cakes dripping with sirupy icings and candied fruits. Once a week, the town band gave a concert in the *Portales.* But every evening, concert or no concert, the young people of the town, between six and seven o'clock, took their evening stroll there.

I had become acquainted with Tomas, son of a dry-goods merchant who had business dealings with my father, and Tomas took me to walk with the other young men of the town in the *Portales,* at the hour when all the girls were out walking, too. But not walking with young men. Oh, no! Not at all. That was unheard of in Toluca. The girls of the better Mexican families merely strolled slowly up and down with their mothers or married sisters, or old aunts, or the family servant, but never unchaperoned or alone.

The boys promenaded in groups of three or four, usually, slowing down when you passed a particular girl you wanted to make an impression on. The girls would always pretend not to notice any of the boys, turning their heads away and giggling and looking in the shop windows. It was not considered polite for a nice girl to really notice boys—although it was all right for the boys to turn and stare at the girls as they went by. So the boys would pause, and look, and then walk on, turning at the end of the walk to retrace their steps until they had covered the three-sided promenade of the *Portales* perhaps fifteen or twenty times an evening. Then suddenly, it would be supper time, and the sidewalks would be deserted. The shops would begin to pull down their zinc shutters, and everybody would go home through the cool mountain darkness to a hot *merienda* of steaming chocolate, tamales, goat's cheese, and buns. And maybe some of the sticky and very sweet cake you had seen in the shop window on the *Portales.*

In Toluca, if a boy fell in love with a girl he could not visit the young lady in her home until he had become engaged to her. He could only go to call on her outside the iron grills of her front window—for all the houses in Toluca had iron grills at the windows to keep lovers and bandits out. Within the living room, back in the shadows somewhere, the chaperon sat, and the lovers would have to speak very low indeed for that attentive female not to hear every word. The boy could hold the girl's hand, and maybe kiss her finger tips—but not often would he be tall enough to steal a kiss from her lips—for most of the windows had a fairly high sill. And even if the girl sat on the floor, through grilled bars and with a vigilant chaperon on the offing, it is not easy to achieve a real kiss.

Good girls in Toluca, as is the custom in very Catholic and very Latin countries, were kept sheltered indeed, both before and after marriage. They did not go into the street alone. They did not come near a man unchaperoned. Girls who worked, servants and typists, and waitresses, and others who ran the streets free, were considered fair game for any man who could make them. But good girls—

between them and the world stood the tall iron bars of *la reja,* those formidable grilled windows of the Latin countries. Sometimes groups of boys in love got together with guitars and went from house to house serenading their sweethearts. And lots of boys wrote poems to their girls and handed the poems, in carefully folded little notes, through the grills for the beloved to read at night in her bed.

But when the mother, or the old aunt, or the family servant decided it was time to close the shutters of *la reja,* the suitor would move on up the street in the dusk, for the shutters usually closed early. Perhaps he would go home, or perhaps he would play a game of *carambola* in the town's one billiard hall. Or perhaps, if he could afford it, he would go to Natcha's house. There were in Toluca two houses of love—one for gentlemen and army officers, the other for Indians and common soldiers. Natcha's house was for gentlemen and officers.

That winter I had begun to teach English in the town—private classes, the mayor's son and daughter and others of the "best" people of Toluca. The Mexican boys envied me getting paid for teaching English to charming young ladies—and some not so young—and for my being permitted to sit in the very room with girls accessible to them only via *la reja.*

Well, that spring one of my pupils fell in love with me. But she was not very young. She was a woman in her thirties to whom I had been giving lessons two afternoons a week. She lived a secluded life with her old aunt—no doubt on a small income. And she had never been married because, since childhood, she had suffered with a heart ailment. She was a very delicate little woman, ivory-tan in color, with a great mass of heavy black hair and very bright but sad eyes. I always thought perhaps she was something like Emily Dickinson, shut away and strange, eager and lonesome, as Emily must have been.

But I had no way of knowing she was going to fall in love with me. She read and spoke a little English, but she wanted to be able to read big novels like Scott and Dickens. Yet she didn't pay much attention to her lessons. When I read aloud, she would look at me—until I looked at her. Then her eyes would fall. After several weeks of classes, shyly, in funny little sentences of awkward English, she finally made me realize she must be in love.

She began to say things like, "Dear Mister, I cannot wait you comeback so long off Friday."

"But you have to learn your verbs," I'd say. "And it will take until Friday."

"The verbs is not much difficult. It's you I am think about, Mister."

She seemed almost elderly to me then, at nineteen. I was confused and didn't know what to say. After a few such sentences in English, she'd blush deeply and take refuge in Spanish. And all I could think of to tell her was that she must not fall in love with me because I was going to New York as soon as I had saved the fare.

The little lady's eyes widened and her face went white when I said it. I thought for a moment she was surely going to faint. And one day she did faint, but it was not, I suppose, about love. It was while we were going over conditionals. Sentences like, "I would write if I could," when she simply keeled over in her chair.

Her old aunt and the servants had told me that that might happen almost anytime. Strains and excitements of any kind upset her. So after that I was never sure as to the safe thing to do when I found her looking at me. She might faint if I held her hand. Or she might faint if I didn't.

But all things end in time. When I came to her house one afternoon at the class hour, I was very sorry (and ashamed at my feeling of relief) to learn that she was quite ill with a heavy cold. She remained abed several days. I took her flowers and sat with her surrounded by little bottles and boxes of pills. When she was better, her aunt carried her away to a lower and warmer climate to convalesce. I never saw her any more. But she wrote me a card once from Cuernavaca, and signed it just, *Maria*.

From: *Opportunity* (April 1940): 107–108.

A CUBAN SCULPTOR

Among the sculptors of the darker world, Ramos Blanco is most certainly deserving of your sincere attention. He is a Cuban Negro, formerly a policeman in the city of Havana where, during his spare hours off duty, he moulded the forms and figures that have lately attracted interest to the amazing promise of this young artist.

He is twenty-nine years old—but already within the last few years his work has been exhibited in France, Italy, and Spain, as well as in his own Cuban island. And in October of this year his monumental statue to heroic black motherhood, *Maternal Heroism,* will be erected in the Parque Medina at Havana, one of the public gardens of the city. This master work of the young Negro sculptor represents, in white marble, the figure of one of the noblest women of the Cuban Revolution, Mariana Granjales, sending her last and youngest son out to die for freedom, after all the other members of her family had been killed by the enemy.

Ramos Blanco spent fourteen months in Italy working on his gigantic monument, for there only could he find the necessary marbles for his creation. While in Rome last spring, a successful exhibition of his works was held in the main galleries of the Casa de España, eliciting much favorable comment from the press of the Italian capital. In no way is this young man's work undeserving of the praise it has received. Its great dignity and simple strength indicate the arrival of a new and interesting personality in the field of American art. And the fact that the first great figure by this dark Cuban sculptor is that of a Negro heroine makes it not without significance to the readers of this magazine—we who have so few memorials to our own racial heroes in this country, so few monuments to Sojourner Truth or Frederick Douglass or Booker Washington or any of the great figures in our own perilous history. It is that we have no artists—or no pride?

From: *Opportunity* 8 (November 1930): 334

Haiti

WHITE SHADOWS IN A BLACK LAND

Imagine a country where the entire national population is colored, and you will have Haiti—the first of the black republics, and that much discussed little land to the South of us. To a Negro coming directly from New York by steamer and landing in Port-au-Prince, the capital, it is like stepping into a new world, a darker world, a world where the white shadows are apparently missing, a world of his own people. The custom officials who examine his baggage will be Negroes, the taxi drivers will be black or brown, his hotel keeper will probably be mulatto. In the shops, clerks of color will wait on him. At the banks, Negroes will cash his travelers' checks and explain the currency of the country to him. Should he visit the Chamber of Deputies, he will find the governing body filled with dark races and even the president of the Republic will have a touch of color in his blood. In the country districts, the peasants who make up the bulk of the population, will smile at him from kind black faces, and the dark visitor from America will feel at home and unafraid.

It is doubly disappointing then, to discover, if you have not already known, how the white shadows have fallen on this land of color. Before you can go ashore, a white American Marine has been on board ship to examine your passport, and maybe you will see a U.S. gunboat at anchor in the harbor. Ashore, you are likely to have run into groups of Marines in the little cafes, talking in "Cracker" accents, and drinking in the usual boisterous American manner. You will discover that the Banque d'Haiti, with its Negro cashiers and tellers, is really under control of the National City Bank of New

York. You will become informed that all the money collected by the Haitian customs passes through the hands of an American comptroller. And regretfully, you will gradually learn that most of the larger stores with their colored clerks are really owned by Frenchmen, Germans, or Assyrian Jews. And if you read the Haitian newspapers, you will soon realize from the heated complaints there, that even in the Chamber of Deputies the strings of government are pulled by white politicians in far-off Washington—and that the American Marines are kept in the country through an illegal treaty thrust upon Haiti by force and never yet ratified by the United States senate. The dark-skinned little Republic, then, has its hair caught in the white fingers of unsympathetic foreigners, and the Haitian people live today under a sort of military dictatorship backed by American guns. They are not free.

But Haiti glories in a splendid history studded with the names of heroes like Toussaint L'Ouverture, Dessalines, and Christophe—great black men who freed their land from slavery and began to work out their own national destinies a full half-century before American Negroes were freed by the Civil War. Under the powerful leadership mentioned above, the French slave-owners were driven from the island, and Haiti became a free country of dark-skinned peoples. Then Christophe built roads and schools, factories and mills. He established laws and constructed a great Citadel on top of a mountain to defend the land and to create a monument in stone that could be seen for many miles away, so that his subjects might look upon it and be proud. That Citadel today, standing in lonely majesty against the clouds twenty miles from the city of Cap Haitien, is still one of the wonders of the New World, and one of the most amazing structures ever built by man. The story of its building, of how thousands of blacks labored at the task of dragging material and heavy bronze cannons up the steep mountain slopes for years, and how the walls gradually began to tower against the sky, is most beautifully told in Vandercook's "Black Majesty," a record of Christophe's life.

But after Christophe's death in 1820, misfortune set in. Revolution after revolution kept the country in turmoil. Politicians and grafters gained control. The Citadel, the palaces, the schools, the roads were left to rack and ruin. The mulattoes and the few blacks with money set themselves apart as an aristocracy, exploited the peasantry, did little to improve the land, and held their heads high in a proud and snobbish manner, not unlike the French masters of old. They sent their children abroad to be educated in the futile upper-class patterns of European culture. Practical work became distasteful to them, physical labor undignified. If one wore shoes, one should not even be seen in the streets carrying a package. Business and commerce were left to foreign initiative. The white shadows began to fall across the land as the dark aristocracy became cultured, and careless, conceited, and quite "high hat." Today, the Marines are there.

From: *The Crisis* 41 (May 1932): 157.

AN APPEAL FOR JACQUES ROMAIN [Sic]

Sir: Jacques Romain, poet and novelist of color, and the finest living Haitian writer, has just been sentenced at Port-au-Prince, Haiti, to two years in jail for circulating there a French magazine of Negro liberation called Cri des Nègres. Jacques Romain is a young man of excellent European education who formerly occupied a high post in the Haitian government and is greatly respected by intellectuals as an outstanding man of letters. He is one of the very few upper-class Haitians who understands and sympathizes with the plight of the oppressed peasants of his island home and who has attempted to write about and to remedy the pitiful conditions of 90 percent of the Haitian people exploited by the big coffee monopolies and by the manipulations of foreign finance in the hands of the National City Bank of New York.

As a fellow writer of color, I call upon all writers and artists of whatever race who believe in the freedom of words and of the human spirit, to protest immediately to the President of Haiti and to the nearest Haitian Consulate the uncalled for and unmerited sentence to prison of Jacques Romain, one of the few, and by far the most talented, of the literary men of Haiti.

From: *The New Republic,* 81 (12 Dec. 1934): 130.

Spain

TOO MUCH OF RACE

Members of the Second International Writers Congress, comrades, and people of Paris: I come from a land whose democracy from the very beginning has been tainted with race prejudice born of slavery, and whose richness has been poured through the narrow channels of greed into the hands of the few. I come to the Second International Writers Congress representing my country, America, but most especially the Negro peoples of America, and the poor peoples of America—because I am both a Negro and poor. And that combination of color and of poverty gives me the right then to speak for the most oppressed group in America, that group that has known so little of American democracy, the fifteen million Negroes who dwell within our borders.

We are the people who have long known in actual practice the meaning of the word Fascism—for the American attitude towards us has always been one of economic and social discrimination: in many states of our country Negroes are not permitted to vote or to hold political office. In some sections freedom of movement is greatly hindered, especially if we happen to be sharecroppers on the cotton farms of the South. All over America we know what it is to be refused admittance to schools and colleges, to theatres and concert halls, to hotels, and restaurants. We know Jim Crow cars, race riots, lynchings, we know the sorrows of the nine Scottsboro boys, innocent young Negroes imprisoned some six years now for a crime that even the trial judge declared them not guilty of having committed, and for which some of them have not yet come to trial.

Yes, we Negroes in America do no have to be told what Fascism is in action. We know. Its theories of Nordic supremacy and economic suppression have long been realities to us.

And now we view it on a world scale: Hitler in Germany with the abolition of labor unions, his tyranny over the Jews, and the sterilization of the Negro children of Cologne; Mussolini in Italy with his banning of Negroes on the theatrical stages, and his expedition of slaughter in Ethiopiá; the Military Party in Japan with their little maps of how they'll conquer the whole world and their savage treatment of Koreans and Chinese; Batista and Vincent, the little American-made tyrants of Cuba and Haiti; and now Spain and Franco with his absurd cry of "Viva España" at the hands of Italians, Moors and Germans invited to help him achieve "Spanish Unity." Absurd, but true.

We Negroes of America are tired of a world divided superficially on the basis of blood and color, but in reality on the basis of poverty and power—the rich over the poor, no matter what their color. We Negroes of America are tired of a world in which it is possible for any group of people to say to another: "You have no right to happiness, or freedom, or the joy of life." We are tired of a world where forever we work for someone else and the profits are not ours. We are tired of a world where, when we raise our voices against oppression, we are immediately jailed, intimidated, beaten, sometimes lynched. Nicolás Guillén has been in prison in Cuba, Jacques Roumain, in Haiti, Angelo Herndon in the United States. Today a letter comes from the great Indian writer, Raj Anand, saying that he cannot be with us here in Paris because the British police in England have taken his passport from him. I say, we darker peoples of the earth are tired of a world in which things like that can happen.

And we see in the tragedy of Spain how far the world oppressors will go to retain their power. To them now the murder of women and children is nothing. Those who have already practiced bombing the little villages of Ethiopia now bomb Guernica and Madrid. The same Fascists who forced Italian peasants to fight in Africa now force African Moors to fight in Europe. They do not care about color when they can use you for profits or for war. Japan attempts to force the Chinese of Manchuria to work and fight under Japanese supervision for the glory and wealth of the Tokyo bourgeoisie—one colored people dominating another at the point of guns. Race means nothing when it can be turned to Fascist use. And yet race means everything when the Fascists of the world use it as a bugaboo and a terror to keep the working masses from getting together. Just as in America they tell the whites that Negroes are dangerous brutes and rapists, so in Germany they lie about Jews, and in Italy they cast their verbal spit upon the Ethiopians. And the old myths of race are kept alive to hurt and impede the rising power of the working class. But in America, where race prejudice is so strong, already we have learned what the lies of race mean—continued oppression and poverty and fear—and now Negroes and white sharecroppers in the cotton fields of the South are beginning to get together; and Negro and white workers in the great industrial cities of the North under John L. Lewis and the C.I.O. have begun to create a great labor force that refuses to recognize the color line. Negro and white stevedores on the docks of the West coast of America have formed one of the most powerful labor unions in America. Formerly the unorganized Negro dockworkers—unorganized because the white workers themselves with their backward ideology didn't permit Negroes in their unions—formerly these Negro workers could break a strike. And they did. But now both Negroes and whites are strong. We are learning.

Why is it that the British police seized Raj Anand's passport? Why is it that the State Department in Washington has not yet granted me permission to go to Spain as a representative of the Negro Press? Why is it that the young Negro leader, Angelo Herndon, was finding it most difficult to secure a passport when I last saw him recently in New York? Why? We know why!

It is because the reactionary and Fascist forces of the world know that writers like Anand and myself, leaders like Herndon, and poets like Guillén and Roumain represent the great longing that is in the hearts of the darker peoples of the world to reach out their hands in friendship and brotherhood to all the white races of the earth. The Fascists know that we long to be rid of hatred and terror and oppression, to be rid of conquering and of being conquered, to be rid of all the ugliness of poverty and imperialism that eat away the heart of life today. We represent the end of race. And the Fascists know that when there is no more race, there will be no more capitalism, and no more war, and no more money for the munition makers, because the workers of the world will have triumphed.

From: *The Volunteer for Liberty,* August 1937; *The Crisis,* September, 1937; *Left Review,* October 1937.

NEGROES IN SPAIN

Madrid

In July, on the boat with me coming from New York, there was a Negro from the far West on his way to Spain as a member of the 9th Ambulance Corps of the American Medical Bureau. He was one of a dozen in his unit of American doctors, nurses, and ambulance drivers offering their services to Spanish democracy.

When I reached Barcelona a few weeks later, in time for my first air raid and the sound of bombs falling on a big city, one of the first people I met was a young Puerto Rican of color acting as interpreter for the Loyalist troops.

A few days later in Valencia, I came across two intelligent young colored men from the West Indies, aviators, who had come to give their services to the fight against Fascism.

And now, in Madrid, Spain's besieged capital, I've met wide-awake Negroes from various parts of the world—New York, our Middle West, the French West Indies, Cuba, Africa—some stationed here, others on leave from their battalions—all of them here because they know that if Fascism creeps across Spain, across Europe, and then across the world, there will be no place left for intelligent young Negroes at all. In fact, no decent place for any Negroes—because Fascism preaches the creed of Nordic supremacy and a world for whites alone.

In Spain, there is no color prejudice. Here in Madrid, heroic and bravest of cities, Madrid where the shells of Franco plow through the roof-tops at night, Madrid where you can take a streetcar to the trenches, this Madrid to whose defense lovers of freedom and democracy all over the world have sent food and money and men— here to this Madrid have come Negroes from all the world to offer their help.

On the opposite side of the trenches with Franco, in the company of the professional soldiers of Germany, and the illiterate troops of Italy, are the deluded and driven Moors of North Africa. An oppressed colonial people of color being used by Fascism to make a colony of Spain. And they are being used ruthlessly, without pity. Young boys, men from the desert, old men, and even women, compose the Moorish hordes brought by the reactionaries from Africa to Europe in their attempt to crush the Spanish people.

I did not know about the Moorish women until, a few days ago, I went to visit a prison hospital here in Madrid filled with wounded prisoners. There were German aviators that bombarded the peaceful village of Colmenar Viejo and machine-gunned helpless women as they fled along the road. One of these aviators spoke English. I asked him why he fired on women and children. He said he was a professional soldier who did what he was told. In another ward, there were Italians who joined the invasion of Spain because they had no jobs at home.

But of all the prisoners, I was most interested in the Moors, who are my own color. Some of them, convalescent, in their white wrappings and their bandages, moved silently like dark shadows down the hall. Others lay quietly suffering in their beds. It was difficult to carry on any sort of conversation with them because they spoke little or no Spanish. But finally, we came across a small boy who had been wounded at the battle of Brunete—he looked to be a child of ten or eleven, a bright smiling child who spoke some Spanish.

"Where did you come from?" I said.

He named a town in Morocco I could not understand.

"And how old are you?"

"Thirteen," he said.

"And how did you happen to be fighting in Spain?"

Then I learned from this child that Franco had brought Moorish women into Spain as well as men—women to wash and cook for the troops.

"What happened to your mother," I said.

The child closed his eyes. "She was killed at Brunete," he answered slowly.

Thus the Moors die in Spain, men, women, and children, victims of Fascism, fighting not for freedom—but against freedom—under a banner that holds only terror and segregation for all the darker peoples of the earth.

A great many Negroes know better. Someday the Moors will know better, too. All the Francos in the world cannot blow out the light of human freedom.

The Volunteer for Liberty, 13 September 1937

LAUGHTER IN MADRID

The thing about living in Madrid these days is that you never know when a shell is going to fall. Or where. Any time is firing time for Franco. Imagine yourself sitting calmly in the front room of your third-floor apartment carefully polishing your eyeglasses when all of a sudden, without the least warning, a shell decides to come through the wall—paying no attention to the open window—and explodes like a thunderclap beneath the sofa. If you are sitting on the sofa, you are out of luck. If you are at the other side of the room and good at dodging shrapnel you may not be killed. Maybe nobody will even be injured in your apartment. Perhaps the shell will simply go on through the floor and kill somebody else in apartment 27, downstairs. (People across the hall have been killed.)

Who next? Where? When? Today all the shells may fall in the Puerta del Sol. Tomorrow Franco's big guns in the hills outside Madrid may decide to change their range-finders and bombard the city fan-wise, sending *quince-y-medios* from one side of the town to the other. No matter in what section of the city you live, a shell may land in the kitchen of the sixth-floor apartment (whose inhabitants you've often passed on the stairs), penetrate several floors, and make its way to the street via your front room on the third floor.

That explains why practically nobody in Madrid bothers to move when the big guns are heard. If you move, you may as likely as not move into the wrong place. A few days ago four shells went through the walls of the Hotel Florida, making twenty that have fallen there. The entrance to the hotel is well protected with sandbags, but they couldn't sandbag nine stories. All this the desk clerk carefully explains to guests who wish to register. But most of the other hotels have been severely bombed, too. And one has to stay somewhere.

The Hotel Alfonso a few blocks away has several large holes through each of its four walls but is still receiving guests. One of the halls on an upper floor leads straight out into space—door and balcony have been shot away. In one of the unused bedrooms you can look slantingly down three floors into the street through the holes made by a shell that struck the roof and plowed its way down, then out by a side wall into the road. Walking up to your room, you pass a point where the marble stairs are splintered and the wall pitted by scraps of iron; here two people were killed. Yet the Hotel Alfonso maintains its staff, and those of its rooms that still have walls and windows are occupied by paying guests.

The now world-famous Telefonica, Madrid's riddled skyscraper in the center of the city, is still standing, proud but ragged, its telephone girls at work inside. The Madrid Post Office has no window-panes left whatsoever, but the mail still goes out. Around the Cibeles Fountain in front of the Post Office the street cars still pass, although the fountain itself with its lovely goddess is now concealed by a specially built housing of bricks and sandbags, so that the good-natured Madrileños have nicknamed it "Beauty Under Covers," laughing at their own wit.

Yes, people still laugh in Madrid. In this astonishing city of bravery and death, where the houses run right up to the trenches and some of the street-car lines stop only at the barricades, people still laugh, children play in the streets, and men buy comic papers as well as war news. The shell holes of the night before are often filled in by dawn, so efficient is the wrecking service and so valiantly do the Madrileños struggle to patch up their city.

A million people living on the front lines of a nation at war! The citizens of Madrid—what are they like? Not long ago a small shell fell in the study of a bearded professor of ancient languages. Frantically his wife and daughter came running to see if anything had happened to him. They found him standing in the center of the floor, holding the shell and shaking his head quizzically. "This little thing," he said, "this inanimate object, can't do us much damage. It's the philosophy that lies behind it, wife, the philosophy that lies behind it."

In the Arguelles quarter to the north, nearest to the rebel lines— the neighborhood that has suffered most from bombardments and air raids—many of the taller apartment houses, conspicuous targets that they are, have been abandoned. But in the smaller houses of one and two stories people still live and go about their tasks. The Cuban poet, Alejo Carpentier, told me that one morning after a heavy shelling he passed a house of which part of the front wall was lying in the yard. A shell had passed through the roof, torn away part of the wall, carried with it the top of the family piano, and buried itself in the garden. Nevertheless, there at the piano sat the young daughter of the house, very clean and starched, her hair brushed and braided, her face shining. Diligently she was beating out a little waltz from a music book in front of her. The fact that the top of the piano had been shot away in the night did not seem to affect the chords. When passers-by asked about it, calling through the shell hole, the child said, "Yes, an *obús* came right through here last night. I'm going to help clean up the yard after a while, but I have to practice my lessons now. My music teacher'll be here at eleven.

The will to live and laugh in Madrid is the thing that constantly amazes a stranger. At the house where I am staying, sometimes a meal consists largely of bread and of soup made with bread. Everybody tightens his belt and grins, and somebody is sure to repeat good-naturedly an old Spanish saying, "Bread with bread—food for fools." Then we all laugh.

One of Franco's ways of getting back at Madrid is to broadcast daily from his radio stations at Burgos and Seville the luncheon and dinner menus of the big hotels, the fine food that the Fascists are eating and the excellent wines they drink. (Rioja and the best of wine areas are in Fascist hands.) But Madrid has ways of getting even with the Fascists, too. Mola, a lover of cafes, said at the very beginning of the war that he would soon be drinking coffee in Madrid. He was mistaken. Then he said he would enter Madrid by the first of November. He didn't. Then he swore he would enter the city on the eighth of December. He didn't. But on the evening of the eighth some wag remembered, and the crowds passing that night in Madrid's darkened Puerta del Sol saw by moonlight in the very center of the square a coffee table, carefully set, the coffee poured, and neatly pinned to the white cloth a large sign reading "For Mola."

Bread and coffee are scarce in Madrid, and so are cigarettes. The only cigarettes offered for sale more or less regularly are small, hard, and very bad. They are so bad that though they cost thirty centimos before the war they bring only twenty now despite their comparative scarcity. The soldiers call them "recruit-killers," jocularly asserting that they are as dangerous to the new men in the army as are bombs and bullets.

Bad cigarettes, poor wine, little bread, no soap, no sugar! Madrid, dressed in bravery and laughter; knowing death and the sound of guns by day and night, but resolved to live, not die!

The moving-picture theaters are crowded. Opening late in the afternoon and compelled to close at nine, they give only one or two showings a day. One evening an audience was following with great interest an American film. Suddenly an *obús* fell in the street outside. There was a tremendous detonation, but nobody moved from his seat. The film went on. Soon another fell, nearer and louder than before, shaking the whole building. The manager went out into the lobby and looked up and down the Gran Via. Overhead he heard the whine of shells. He went inside and mounted the stage to say that, in view of the shelling, he thought it best to stop the picture. Before he had got the words out of his mouth he was greeted with such a hissing and booing and stamping of feet and calls for the show to go on that he shrugged his shoulders in resignation and signaled the operator to continue. The house was darkened. The magic of Hollywood resumed its spell. While Franco's shells whistled dangerously over the theater, the film went its make-believe way to a thrilling denouement. The picture was called "Terror in Chicago."

From: *The Nation* 146 (29 January 1938): 123–24.

ESSAYS FROM THE AFRO-AMERICAN

HUGHES BOMBED IN SPAIN: TELLS OF
TERROR OF FASCIST RAID
Women, Children Huddled in Fear
as Bombs Explode

By Langston Hughes

Madrid

I came down from Paris by train. We reached Barcelona at night.
The day before there had been a terrific air raid in the city, killing
almost a hundred persons in their houses and wounding a great many
more. We read about it in the papers at the border: AIR RAID
OVER BARCELONA.

"Last night!" I thought, "Well, tonight I'll be there."

There's a tunnel between France and Spain, a long stretch of
darkness through which the trains pass. Then you come out into the
sunlight again directly into the village of Port Bou on the Spanish
side of the mountain, with a shining blue bay below where children
are swimming.

But as you leave the train, you notice that the windows of the
station are almost all broken. Several nearby houses are in ruins,
gutted by bombs. And in the winding streets of the village there are
signs, REFUGIO, pointing to holes in the mountains in case of air-
raids. That is wartime Spain. A little town by the blue Mediterranean
where travellers change trains.

In the country they were harvesting the wheat land, as we rode
southward, we saw men and women working with their scythes in the
fields. The Barcelona train was very crowded. I was travelling with
Nicolás Guillén, the colored poet from Havana, and a Mexican
writer and his wife.

They kept up a rapid fire of Spanish in various accents all around
me. Guillén and I were the only colored on the train, so I thought,
until at one of the stations when we got out to buy fruit, we noticed a
dark face leaning from the window of the coach ahead of us. When
the train started again, we went forward to investigate.

He was a young brown-skin boy from the Canary Islands. He wore a red shirt and blue beret. He had escaped from the fascists who now control his island by the simple expedient of getting into his fishing boat with the rest of her crew and sailing toward Africa.

The Canary Islands belong to Spain, but the fisherman do not like the fascists who have usurped power there, and so many of them sail their boats away and come to fight on the mainland with the Spanish government. This young man had come to fight.

He spoke a strange Spanish dialect which was hard for us to understand, but he made it clear to us that he did not like fascism with its crushing of the labor unions and the rights of working people like himself. He told us that a great many folks who live in the Canary Islands are colored, mixed with African and Spanish blood.

It was almost midnight when we got to Barcelona. There were no lights in the town, and we came out of the station into pitch darkness. A bus took us to the hotel. It was a large hotel several stories high which, before the Civil War, had been a fashionable stopping place for tourists.

We had rooms on an upper floor. The desk clerk said that in case of air-raids we might come down into the lobby, but that a few floors more or less wouldn't make much difference. The raids were announced by a siren, but guests would be warned by telephone as well. That night there was no bombing, so we slept in peace.

The next day Guillén and I were sitting in a side-walk cafe on the tree-lined boulevard called Las Ramblas, when a dark young colored man came by.

He looked at us, then turned and spoke. He recognized me, he said, because he had heard me speak in New York. He was a Puerto Rican who had come from Harlem to serve as interpreter in Spain. His name was Roldan. He invited us to go with him to the Mella Club where Cubans and West Indians gather in Barcelona.

The Mella Club, named after Julio Antonio Mella, famous Cuban student leader assassinated in Mexico, occupies the whole second floor of a large building near the center of the town. It has a beautiful courtyard for games and dancing, and a little bar where Cuban drinks are mixed. We were invited to a dance that afternoon given in honor of the soldiers on leave, and here we met a number of Cubans, both colored and white, and a colored Portuguese, all taking an active part in the Spanish struggle against the fascists.

And all of them finding in loyalist Spain more freedom than they had known at home—for most of the West Indian Islands are burdened by colonial or semi-fascistic types of dictatorships such as Batista's in Cuba, and Vincent's in Haiti. And all of them draw the color-line between colored and whites.

In Spain, as one could see at the dance that afternoon, there is no color line, and Catalonian girls and their escorts mingled gaily with the colored guests.

That night, back at the hotel, one knew that it was war-time because, in the luxurious dining room with its tuxedoed waiters, there was only one fixed dinner menu, no choice of food. It was a good dinner of soup, fish, meat, one vegetable, and fruit, but nothing elaborate. Later, as one often does in Europe, we went to a sidewalk cafe for coffee.

Until midnight, we sat at our table watching the crowd strolling up and down the broad Ramblas. The fact that Barcelona was lightless did not seem to keep people home on a warm evening. A few wan bulbs from the interior of the cafes cast a dull glow on the sidewalks, but that was the only visible light, save for the stars shining brightly above.

The buildings were great grey shadows towering in the night, with windows shuttered and curtains drawn. There must be no light on any upper floors to guide enemy aviators.

At midnight, the public radios began to blare forth the war-news, and people gathered in large groups on corners to hear it. Then the cafe closed and we went to the hotel. I had just barely gotten to my room and had begun to undress when the low extended wail of the siren began, letting us know that the fascist planes were coming. (They come from Mallorca across the sea at a terrific speed, drop their bombs, and circle away into the night again.)

Quickly, I put on my shirt, passed Guillén's room, and together we started downstairs. Suddenly all the lights went out in the hotel, but we heard people rushing down the halls and stairways in the dark. A few had flashlights with them to find the way. Some were visibly frightened. In the lobby two candles were burning, casting weird, giantlike shadows on the walls.

In an ever increasing wail the siren sounded louder and louder, droning its deathly warning. Suddenly it stopped. By then the lobby was full of people, men, women, and children, speaking in Spanish,

English, and French. In the distance we heard a series of quick explosives.

"Bombs?" I asked.

"No, anti-aircraft gun," a man explained.

Everyone was very quiet. Then we heard the guns go off again.

"Come here," the man called, leading the way. Several of us went out on the balcony where, in the dark, we could see the searchlights playing across the sky. Little round puffs of smoke from the anti-aircraft shells floated against the stars. In the street a few women hurried along to public bomb-proof cellars.

Then for a long while nothing happened. After about an hour, the lights suddenly came on in the hotel again as a signal that the danger had ended. Evidently, the enemy planes had been driven away without having dropped any bombs. Everyone went back upstairs to bed. The night was quiet again. I put out my light, opened the window, and went to sleep.

Being very tired, I slept soundly without dreaming. The next thing I knew, the telephone was ringing violently in the dark, the siren screaming its long blood-curdling cry again, and the walls of the building shaking.

BOOM! Then the dull roar of a dying vibration. And another BOOM! Through my window I saw a flash of light. I didn't stay to look again. Down the hall I went, clothes in my arms, sensing my way toward the staircase in the dark.

This time the air-raid was on for sure. When I got to the lobby, the same people as before were gathered there in various stages of dress and undress. Children crying, women talking hysterically, men very quiet. Nobody went out on the balcony now.

In the street an ambulance passed, its bell ringing into the distance. The anti-aircraft guns kept up their rapid fire. The last BOOM of the enemy bombs was a long way off. The planes, with their cargo of death partially emptied, were driven away. But for a long time nobody left the lobby.

When I went back to bed, dawn was coming in at my open window. Below, in the cool light, the rooftops of Barcelona were grey and lonely. Soon a little breeze blew in from the sea and the red of the rising sun stained the sky. I covered up my head to keep out the light, but I couldn't go to sleep for a long time.

The Afro-American, 23 October 1937

HUGHES FINDS MOORS BEING USED AS PAWNS
BY FASCISTS IN SPAIN:
Colored Sympathizers from Many Lands, However, Aiding
People's Army; Ox-Carts Still Used in Rural Areas

By Langston Hughes

Madrid

Down through the Catalonian country-side our car went speeding, through villages as old as the Romans, and out along the Mediterranean, bright and blue as the morning sky. Straight across the Mediterranean, Italy. To the North, France. And here, Spain. The Latin lands, Italy, fascist. France, democratic. Spain torn between fascism and democracy.

Why had I come to Spain? To write for the colored press. I knew that Spain once belonged to the Moors, a colored people ranging from light dark to dark white. Now the Moors have come again to Spain with the fascist armies as cannon fodder for Franco. But, on the loyalist side there are many colored people of various nationalities in the International Brigades. I want to write about both Moors and colored people.

I sat comfortably in the back seat of the car beside that excellent colored writer, Nicolás Guillén, who had come from Cuba, representing Mediodia, of which he is the editor. We were headed South to Valencia on the way from Barcelona, the night after an air-raid, driving through fields of wheat and groves of olives and oranges, and cities that recently had been bombed from the air or shelled from the sea. And as the tragic and beautiful landscape went by, I began to think back over the first stages of my trip to Spain.

I came from California and the writing of an opera with Grant Still. I sailed alone on the Aquitania from New York, but once on board, I found several people that I knew. Among them, Mary Church Terrell from Washington, who was sailing for London to deliver a speech on "The Progress and Problems of Colored Women" before the International Assembly of the World Fellowship of Faith.

She presented me to Bishop J. A. Hamleft and his wife, of Kansas City, who were going to Oxford to attend the World Conference of the Universal Christian Council where, they said, other colored churchmen in attendance would include Dr. Mays of Howard

University, Dr. King of Gammon, Bishop Ransom, and Bishop Kyles.

Washington was indeed well represented on shipboard. Mrs. Lorenzo Turner was London bound to join her husband, Dr. Turner of the English Department at Fisk. Mrs. Marie B. Schanks, engaged in juvenile work for the District of Columbia Police Department, was vacationing in England, France, Holland, and Belgium, with Mrs. Kathryn Cameron Brown, teacher of sciences in Washington, and Mrs. E. T. Fields of Chattanooga. Miss Catherine Grigsby, also of the capital, was bound for a summer course at the University of Paris.

Altogether, a large and representative group of colored people— some sailing for cultural and Christian missions, some for study, some for pleasure.

But, in addition, there were four of us going to Spain: myself as a writer; two young men in third class who did not announce their destination; but whom I later met in Spain—aviators from one of the Caribbean Islands; and finally, C. G. Carter, formerly a student in the School of Medicine at the University of Minnesota.

He was the only colored person among the members of the Ninth Medical Unit of the American Medical Bureau to Aid Spanish Democracy, also sailing on the Aquitania. The twelve members of the unit, in their trim uniforms, made an attractive and interesting group.

The American Medical Bureau has sent to Spain more than a hundred doctors and nurses, five hundred beds, great quantities of hospital material, and over thirty ambulances. In their selection of doctors, nurses, and assistants, they have not drawn the color-line, and at least one colored nurse, Salaria Kee of Harlem, has come to Spain under their auspices. And there are several colored ambulance drivers.

So far, I believe, there are no colored doctors in Spain, but the bureau would welcome the participation of colored physicians in their work, so the doctor in charge of the Ninth Unit assured me.

Carter, who hails from Ogden, Utah, attracted a great deal of attention on the boat, dressed in his khaki-colored uniform. The nurses wore long blue capes and blue caps. Carter told me that he found them a fine group of people to travel with and that, although one of the nurses was from the South, she proved to be a splendid and friendly person.

This Ninth American Medical Unit was in charge of Dr. S. N. [Sic] Franklin of Milwaukee and was composed, besides Dr. Franklin, of one x-ray man, one dental technician, six graduate nurses, two ambulance drivers, and one mechanic. They had sent ahead of them four ambulances, two trucks, and a large supply of blankets, sheets, surgical instruments, and canned goods, as well as automatic washing-machines, dryers, and other apparatus for the establishment of a modern hospital laundry.

Their unit included two Catholics, as well as members of the Protestant and Jewish faiths. They were going to Spain for humanitarian work in government territory, and seemed to be delighted to have a colored person among them as a co-worker.

When I saw Carter a few weeks later in Spain, he told me that he had learned more in the short time he had been abroad than he had in all the thirty-odd years of his life in the States put together.

"Spain is a fine country," he said. "I hope these people win their war. Mussolini wants to take over Spain just as he did Ethiopia, but the way these people feel, I don't think he's going to do it. Who wants to be a slave to Mussolini?"

As our car sped southward toward Valencia that sunny morning, when I stopped thinking back over my trip to look out the window, I could see quite plainly for myself that the Spanish people didn't want to be enslaved to anyone, native or foreign.

As we passed, peasants in the fields lifted their clenched fists in the government salute. On walls ruined by fascist bombardments, slogans were freshly painted hailing the People's Army. In the villages, young men were drilling to go to the front.

The beautiful landscapes of Spain rolled by as our car went down the road, the Spain that now for more than a year has occupied the headlines on the front pages of the world. The Spain of the huge meetings I had attended at home, with three and four thousand dollar collections given for food and medical supplies, and milk for babies.

The new democratic Spain that I had seen placarded in the main streets of cities like Denver and Salt Lake City when I lectured there. AID REPUBLICAN SPAIN! MILK FOR THE BABIES OF SPANISH DEMOCRACY! The Spain for which Josephine Baker in Paris had danced at a benefit for child refugees; and for which Paul Robeson had sung in London.

A colored band, too, from the Paris Moulin Rouge had played in honor of the Second International Writers Congress just returned to France from Madrid, having in attendance the French African writer, René Maran, the French West Indian poet, Leon Damas, and the Haitian poet, Jacques Roumain, as well as Nicolás Guillén and myself—five colored writers, each from a different part of the world.

Within the last year, colored people from many different countries have sent men, money, and sympathy to Spain in her fight against the forces that have raped Ethiopia, and that clearly hold no good for any poor and defenseless people anywhere. Not only artists and writers with well-known names, the Paul Robesons and René Marans of international fame, but ordinary colored people like those I met in the Cuban club in Barcelona, and like Carter, the ambulance driver, or the nurse from Harlem! These especially are the people I want to write about in Spain.

Naturally, I am interested in the Moors, too, and what I can find out about them. As usually happens with colored troops in the service of white imperialists, the Moors have been put in the front lines of the Franco offensive in Spain—and shot down like flies. They have been brought by the thousands from Spanish Morocco where the fascists took over power in the early days of their uprising.

First, the regular Moorish cavalry and guard units came to Spain, then civilian conscripts forced into the army, or deceived by false promises of loot and high pay. When they got to Spain, as reputable newspaper correspondents have already written, they were often paid off in worthless German marks which they were told would be good to spend when they got back to Africa.

But most of the Moors never live to get back to Africa. Now, in the second year of the war, they are no longer a potent force in Franco's army. Too many of them have been killed!

What I sought to find out in Spain was what effect, if any, this bringing of dark troops to Europe had had on the Spanish people in regard to their racial feelings. Had prejudice and hatred been created in a land that did not know it before? What has been the treatment of Moorish prisoners by the loyalists? Are they segregated and ill-treated? Are there any Moors on the government side?

As I thought of these things, our car began to slow down and I noticed that the traffic had grown heavier on the road. Burros, trucks, and ox-carts mingled in long lines of dust. Fords and oxen, the old and the new! Peasants on mule-back, soldiers in enormous

American-made trucks. On either side of us there were orange groves as far as one could see. And in the distance, tall medieval towers mingled with modern structures. We were approaching a city, a big city. "Valencia," the chauffeur said.

Valencia, ancient Mediterranean seaport, and now the seat of the Spanish government. I had been there twelve years ago as a sailor in the days when there was a king on the throne in Spain. Now, the people themselves are in power and democracy prevails—except that the rich, the generals, and the former friends of the king are trying to smash this democracy and have hired Franco to put the country back in chains again.

To help them do this, they called in professional soldiers, Italians, Germans, and Moors, to crush the duly elected government. Only four regiments of the regular army remained with the government, so the government had to form its own army, the People's Army, made up of farmers and working men.

To help this People's Army, and to fight fascism before it makes any further gains in the world, men came to Spain from all over the earth. They formed the International Brigades. In these brigades there are many colored people. To learn about them, I came to Spain.

The Afro-American, 30 October 1937

"ORGAN GRINDER'S SWING" HEARD ABOVE
GUNFIRE IN SPAIN—HUGHES
Lunceford, Calloway and Ellington
Already Known There; Ability,
Not Color Found to Count Most

By Langston Hughes

Madrid

Colored people are not strange to Spain, nor do they attract an undue amount of attention.

In small villages, they may or may not be the center of friendly curiosity for a while, depending on whether or not the villagers have seen a colored face before. But most Spaniards have seen colored faces. In the first place, many Spaniards are quite dark themselves, particularly those from the South, where the sun is hot and Africa not far away. Distinct traces of Moorish blood still remain.

Copper-colored gypsies, too, are common everywhere. In Mexico, I once saw a Spanish bullfighter who was what Harlem would call brownskin. And since I've been in Spain, I've seen plenty of Spanish Spaniards who couldn't possibly pass for white in the States—except that their hair is usually straight.

There seem to be quite a number of colored Portuguese living in Spain. I've met them in both Valencia and Madrid. And in both cities, too, I've seen pure-blooded Africans from the Spanish colonies. Not to mention the Cubans who, especially since the oppressive dictatorships in their homeland have migrated to the Iberian peninsula.

All the colored people of whatever nationality to whom I've talked in Spain agree that there is not the slightest trace of color-prejudice to be found. In that respect, Spain is even better than France, because in Paris, charming city that it is, some of the big hotels catering to American and English tourists are a bit snooty about receiving dark-skinned guests.

In Valencia I talked to a young medical student from Spanish Guinea. He was a pure African, educated in Spain. I saw him at the beach one Sunday afternoon bathing with a group of Spanish friends, young men and women. Thinking perhaps he was an

American or West Indian from one of the International Brigades, I went up to him to inquire.

When he learned that I came from the United States he immediately asked me about Harlem. He said he had heard a great deal about Harlem, and he hoped to go there to visit sometime.

"To stay?" I asked him.

"I don't think I want to stay," he said. "I like Spain, but I want to see Harlem."

He told me that he was a member of the People's Army and because he had been a university student, he was studying for an officership. He said he had not heard from his parents in Africa for more than a year, since the Fascists were in control of the Spanish colonies, and no mail came through any more.

I asked him what he thought about the war and Spain's People's Front government.

He said:

"I really want the government to win the war. They stand for a liberal colonial policy with a chance for the people in Africa to develop and become educated. On the other side with the Fascists are all the old dukes and counts and traders who have exploited the colonies so long for their own benefit, without giving anything back to the people.

"The generals on Franco's side don't even want their own Spanish peasants to escape from serfdom, let alone us in Africa. The same Italians who dropped bombs on Ethiopia have come over here to help Franco bomb the Spaniards!"

"That's right," I said. "I wish I had some paper, I'd interview you for the colored readers in America."

But we were in our bathing suits on the crowded Valencia beach on a Sunday afternoon—which is like Coney Island, and not a very convenient place for an extended conversation. The African student-soldier promised to come to my hotel later in the week for my requested interview, but before the appointed day, I left for Madrid.

Transportation being difficult to find, since there are no trains to the interior, I had to take the first chance opportunity offered me. I would've liked to talk more with the Spanish African boy, and perhaps I can when I return to Valencia.

In Madrid, as I learned shortly after my arrival, one of the most popular of theatrical stars in the city is El Negro Aquilino, now in his third month at the Calderon Theatre, a leading Spanish vaudeville house. Colored jazz bands and performers both from Cuba and the United States have always been very well received in Spain, and colored performers whom I met in Paris told me that in normal times they enjoyed playing in Spain, and that they found the audiences most cordial.

Aquilino, a Cuban, has been here for some time, right through the worst of the war days, and is a great favorite with the soldiers for whom he often performs at the front.

As for jazz in Spain as in all Europe, it is very well liked, and Spanish orchestras do better at playing hot music in the true style than do most bands of other European nations. In normal times, records by Duke Ellington and Cab Calloway sell in large numbers here.

Now, they are exhausted and no new ones are arriving, but they are to be heard frequently by transcription on the air. In fact, during one of the heavy shellings of Madrid a few nights ago, a shell from one of Franco's cannon fell crashing into the street at our corner just as our radio in the dining room began to play Jimmie Lunceford's version of "Organ Grinder's Swing!"

Paul Robeson's British-made picture, "Song of Freedom," with Nina Mae McKinney, has been playing lately at the neighborhood theatres, and the Madrileños are hoping he will come to loyalist Spain to sing in person. They like him.

As for books, the least representative of the books on colored people seem to be the only ones translated into Spanish—or rather perhaps I should say, the most sensational and exotic. Seabrook's "Magic Island," Peterkin's "Scarlet Sister Mary," Paul Morand's bad short stories of stavism. And nothing by colored writers themselves.

Walter White's "Fire in the Fling," for instance, or James Weldon Johnson's "Along This Way," would be of greatest interest to Spanish readers just now, struggling as they are with tremendous social problems of their own. However, because of the war, very few books are being published at present in Spain, and the old ones still sold in the shops are typical of the money-making commercialism of former days.

The People's Front government will, no doubt, now that the publishing houses belong to the unions themselves in most cases, improve the selection of foreign books chosen for publication in Spain.

The only representative books on colored people to be found in Madrid now are Blaise Cendar's African anthology, and an excellent anthology of Spanish-American Negro poetry edited by the Cuban poet, Emilio Ballagas of Havana. It is called "Antologia de Poesía Negra," and contains the best of the poems written by or about colored people in the Spanish language.

Tap-dancing is quite popular, and whenever colored dancers are seen in the movies, Spanish youngsters try their best to imitate their steps—and do pretty well, too, because the Spanish sense of rhythm is not at all bad.

Among Madrid sports lovers, talk of the last Olympic games and the exploits of Jesse Owens and the other dark stars therein has not yet died down. Their amazing performances in that most Aryan of all lands—Germany—cause the Spaniards to continue to laugh with glee—since Hitler is none too popular here anyway, considering all the bombing planes he has sent to the Spanish fascists to be used against the working people.

Old-timers still remember Jack Johnson and his exhibition bouts in Madrid years ago. And they say that a colored fighter who once boxed with him is still living here but, so far, I've been unable to locate him. If I do, he's in for an interview and a picture.

But in Spain, the most interesting colored people one meets—at the front or on Madrid's Gran Via—are not prize fighters, or writers, or performers in the theatres.

They're men with uniforms on, khaki-colored uniforms, and the insignia of various regiments. Men from St. Louis, Chicago, Harlem, Panama City, Havana. Those you never heard of in any book. (But you will, in due time, no doubt.) They're in the International Brigade.

And they're just people from the various corners of the world who've come to help the "just people" of Spain in their fight with the folks with the big names—folks like the Duke of Alba, General Francisco Franco, and Il Duce.

The Afro-American, 6 November 1937

MADRID GETTING USED TO BOMBS; IT'S FOOD SHORTAGE THAT HURTS:
Streets Crowded During Day, Deserted at Night; Sugar, Bread Scarce; Can't Buy Cigarettes

By Langston Hughes

Madrid

Today the Fascists are shelling Madrid again. The shells from their big guns exploding as they strike and the sound of crumbling plaster can be heard quite clearly as I write. In fact, "clearly" is not the word. Loud and near would be a better description of their sounds.

The house where I live has only been struck once, and then not by a direct hit. A shell fell one night just across the street, killing two lovers who were standing in a doorway, and the shrapnel broke our windows and nicked the brick of our walls—so that now our house looks as if it had had smallpox.

Today the shells sound as if they might be falling in the midtown region, which means that street cars crowded with people (for it is the afternoon rush hour) may be hit, and dozens killed and wounded.

The street car men of Madrid, by the way, have often been written of as splendid examples of civilian bravery under fire. Their cars continue to run, bombardments or not. There is no way of telling where the shells are going to fall—in the street or on the houses, on the east side of town or on the west side, in the suburbs or in the heart of the city—so why stop the street cars?

Sometimes a car is struck; yes, but if one took to shelter, the shelter might be hit, too. Besides, most Madrileños have become so used to shellings that they seldom alter their plans on account of cannon fire, and if they have some place to go at a time when shells are falling, they start, anyway—although on the road they may have to take sudden refuge in a courtyard, or a subway station.

Mothers in the more dangerous sections of town usually call their children at the sound of the first boom of the cannon. But the children are often more expert than the grown-ups in recognizing the sounds of artillery and from which direction the shells are coming.

"Aw, those are our cannons, ma. The Fascists haven't started firing yet." I heard a small boy yell from the street to his mother in the window one day, as he kept on playing.

Frequently, late at night or rather very early in the morning for three or four o'clock seems to be the favorite hours for Franco, the crash of shells on nearby pavements or roof-tops will cause you to open your eyes, forget all about sleep, and wonder whether the next shell intends to fall in your bedroom. That is, if you haven't been in Madrid very long.

The Madrileños, however, unless the shelling is very heavy, seldom even wake up any more. If the bombardment is a long one, and several guns are dropping missiles of death on the town, then people may get out of bed and seek the basement, particularly if the aim is directed toward one's own neighborhood.

There are certain sections of Madrid, so they say, that are more dangerous than the actual trenches, for they are wide open to artillery fire. Between the Fascist cannons and the aviation, whole districts of Madrid have been quite destroyed, and people can no longer live in them.

The beautiful Arguelles section of modern apartment houses is nothing but a shambles of broken walls and floorless houses. One enormous apartment house, covering a whole city block, and known as the House of Flowers, because in the planning of it each balcony had its window-box or row of potted vines and plants—this formerly lovely dwelling place is empty and desolate, its tenants dead or scattered, great shell holes in its walls, and the huge rents of aviation bombs in its roofs.

In the center of the city, scarcely a store or office building has not, at one time or another during the past year, been hit by either aviation or shell fire. The world-famous Telefónica, American built center of Spain's telephones (and Madrid's main switchboard) has more than a hundred shell holes in the walls of its twelve stories—yet the telephone service continues to function.

The upper floors, however, are no longer in use, as its tower still serves as a target for Franco's gunners. Since Madrid sits on a raised plateau, and the Telefónica is the highest building in Madrid, it can be seen easily from any of the surrounding Fascist positions.

The hotel where the famous American writer, Ernest Hemingway lives, has also been the object of frequent shelling. Its lower floor is well-protected by sandbags, but it is impossible to sandbag a whole building. From its upper floors, one can look through shell holes on a bird's-eye view of Madrid and the nearby Fascist territory.

To a stranger arriving in Spain's capital city for the first time, it seems strange and amazing to see people going calmly about their business in the streets, the theatres and cafes open, the street car lines running right up to the barricades and the trenches.

But then when night comes and no street lights are lighted as dusk falls, the visiting stranger begins to realize that he is in a war zone. Then if a battle begins in one of the sectors of the city, he realizes that not only is he in a war zone, but at the very front itself. The crack of rifle fire, the staccato run of the machine-guns, and the boom of trench mortars and hand-grenades can be heard so clearly that one finally realizes the war is only a few blocks away.

But no doubt before the night is over, Fascist artillery will begin to drop shells on the town, and then the visitor to Madrid is not only near the war, but in it. Madrid is a city under fire, itself a front-line trench.

But not only shells and the sound of shells make one know that Madrid is at war. There are other signs. In the hotels there is no choice of food at meals, only one menu. In the streets, one notices long lines in front of certain food stores, particularly those for milk and meat.

Sometimes a restaurant will have no bread, or a cafe no sugar for the coffee. Cigars and cigarettes are impossible to buy. A great deal of the shortage of food in Madrid is due to the fact that there is no train service of any kind into the city.

In spite of the difficulties of living in Madrid at present, and those difficulties are many: war and death at one's door, a monotonous and limited diet, soap and cigarettes impossible to find, no heat in the houses—in spite of all this, the people of Madrid are calm, serene, even gay at times with flashes of the old gaiety for which Madrid was noted among the capitals of Europe before the war.

Every day the streets are crowded with soldiers in from the trenches on leave. Sundays, the town-folks, too, are walking on the Gran Via, or up and down the tree-lined boulevards.

Cafes are lively. Long lines wait in front of the theatres for tickets. Special meetings in honor of some brigade, or to report on some phase of the country's problems, are crowded to the doors. Concerts and exhibits are packed. During a shelling, the streets become less crowded for awhile, but as soon as the big guns stop, people are out again.

To foreigners, the Spaniards are most hospitable and helpful. They often turn and accompany a stranger to his destination, if he stops bewildered to ask the way. Their precious cigarettes, when they have them, they will share on the shortest acquaintance. Generosity seems to be a national characteristic.

One day I stopped at a shoe shop to get a loose sole sewn on. The shoemaker fixed the shoe for me, a ten-minute job, and when I asked him how much it would be, his reply was, "Nothing! That's all right! Nothing."

Another day, I passed a family eating long slices of Persian melon in their doorway. They had seen me pass before and knew that I was a stranger. This time, the old grandmother called me and held out a slice of melon. "We're poor, but we have good hearts," she said. "Take this with you."

For those foreigners who've remained in Spain helping the people during the war, or for those who approach their problems with sympathy, nothing is too good. In this respect, the Spanish common people are like those of Russia, where the average worker seems proud to be able to show hospitality to any visitor to the workers' republic.

To colored visitors, the Spaniards are just as hospitable as to any others. And many of them are interested in discussing the problems of colored people in America, having read so often of the lynchings held in our country. They do not, however, realize the extent of the economic and social discrimination which we have to face, and when I tell them about jim-crow theatres, trains, jobs, and schools, they wonder, since there are fifteen million of us, why we don't do something radical about it.

They often ask me, too, concerning the labor movement in America, and whether the colored people are a part of the CIO that is now so often mentioned in the European papers.

Then I ask about their war and whether they think they will win. And, of course, they do. That is what makes Madrid so entirely calm and brave in the face of the guns, and the almost daily bombardments. They say that Franco has no men who believe in him—only hired troops, conscripted Moors, and borrowed Germans and Italians.

They say that he holds his conquered territory only by terror, by the execution of all the workers and intellectuals who oppose him, and by the forming of huge concentration camps. They know that the international situation is becoming more and more favorable to loyalist Spain. And that the government forces are now stronger and better than ever, with greater supplies of material and thousands of well-disciplined men at their command.

Time is with the people of Spain. Time, and the moral consciousness of the world.

The Fascists who bomb women and children, who have put to death García Lorca, Spain's greatest poet, who deliberately rained explosives on the art museum of El Prado and on the National Library with its priceless books and manuscripts, who use churches for arsenals and bring Mohammedans to battle for a "Christian ideal," and who fight for no cause at all except the forcing of the Spanish people back into economic and spiritual slavery for the sake of a handful of rich men and outworn nobles—these Fascists, Madrid feels, cannot win.

Let them pour a million foreign-made shells into the city, they cannot win! Even a great many of the workers of the countries that make the shells for Franco do not want Franco to win.

Sometimes a shell falls that does not explode. And sometimes in such a shell a note is found: This shell will not go off! Greetings! Signed: A German Worker.

The Afro-American, 20 November 1937

MADRID'S FLOWERS HOIST BLOOMS
TO MEET RAINING FASCIST BOMBS:
Soldiers Go to School in Trenches, Which Zig-zag
Through Gardens, and Shell-Torn Homes

By Langston Hughes

Madrid

A few days ago, I went to visit a section of the trenches of Madrid that runs through one of the formerly populous working-class suburbs of the city. Ordinarily, from the center of the town, one can walk to the trenches, but this particular sector was a bit far, so we went in a car, myself and two other foreign writers.

In less than five minutes from the Puerta del Sol, we passed the first barricades built across the road. And soon another set of barricades.

Then we entered a section of the city that had been evacuated where nobody lived any longer. Here the houses, most of them, were in various stages of destruction. Some of the buildings had been completely gutted by bombs from the fascist planes. Others had great ragged holes in their front walls from shell fire.

In third- and fourth-floor tenements, one could see the humble furniture of the former inhabitants still there: a bed with weather-stained mattress, a washstand with the mirror broken by bullets, a bath tub still clinging to the wall although the door is gone.

On the railings of some of the balconies, flowers still bloomed in red pots that the guns had missed.

Ruined and lifeless cities are very sad. I've seen them in Mexico. And I've seen what remained of Chapai after the Japanese bombarded it in their attack on Chinese Shanghai some years ago. And lately I've seen Arguelles, that ruined section of Madrid proper which faces the fascist cannon and was the target of so much foreign aviation last fall and winter.

The district through which I passed on my way to the trenches was not unlike Arguelles in appearance, or Chapai; roofless houses, walless buildings, peopleless homes.

Here there had been hand to hand fighting in those November days when the fascists had entered the very city of Madrid itself, only to be thrown back—never, so the people say now, to enter again.

The ruins through which I passed remain as a reminder of the death and destruction which the fascists created during their attack, an attack repelled by working people, many of them armed only with courage, because a year ago Madrid itself did not have the arms or the trained soldiers which it now has to defend itself.

Nevertheless, the traitorous army of Franco with its Italian and Moorish mercenaries, met with one of the most heroic examples of mass resistance in the history of modern warfare, and were forced to retreat beyond the edges of the city. Now I was going to see a section of those trenches which serve as Madrid's present line of defense.

The tall ruined buildings gave way to smaller buildings, and then to brick and stucco houses with yards about them and what had once been gardens. We were approaching the open country. But here our car stopped because it was dangerous to drive any further.

We got out and went to staff headquarters and presented our papers. The commandant was most cordial, and sent an officer and an aide to guide us through the trenches. Here began one of the strangest and most fantastic tours I have ever made in my life.

For awhile we walked down what would have been in normal times a suburban street, but now nobody lived in the houses we passed. Empty and shell-scarred, they stood in the afternoon sunlight.

Many of the walls were chipped by the marks of recent bullets, because we were now in range of enemy machine-gun and rifle fire. The trunks of the trees were broken and scarred by bullets.

Shells and trench-mortars had made deep holes in some of the lawns where scanty grass still tried to grow. No birds sang in the trees. They had all been frightened away months ago.

We came to the beginning of our rear line of trenches which started modestly enough in a slight rise of land and deepened as the slope went upward.

But the strange thing to me about these trenches was that they were not long straight lines such as we see in the war-movies.

Instead they curved and zig-zagged through gardens, under fences, and beneath houses. Or sometimes they passed right through the wall and living room of a cottage, or maybe through the whole house, past the stove in the kitchen and then on out of doors to become an open trench again.

Like frightful modernistic drawings, the mangled houses lifted their broken walls and torn roofs to the cool blue sky, and trenches cut through rooms where once families had lived and children had played. In one house, or rather a portion of a house—for one whole side had been blown away—we paused and were shown up a broken staircase to the second floor.

Here, through a sand-bagged window, we could get an excellent view of the fascist lines a few hundred yards away. The scattered houses on the furthest edge of the suburb were in fascist territory. Like as not, I thought, newspaper men from Rome and Berlin come down here to this fascist front and peer out of those houses at us in Madrid!

But we went even closer to rebel territory! Our own front-line trenches were nearer yet. And because it was a quiet afternoon, with practically no firing going on, we were allowed to visit them. There was a cold wind blowing, and the soldiers were, many of them wrapped in blankets as they stood at their posts.

They gave us a courteous "Salud!" Not salute, but s-a-l-u-d, spoken in a friendly voice. Sometimes they let us look through their gun-sights toward the enemy. Sometimes we stopped to talk with a group of them in their dugouts, men off duty and at rest.

The trenches were very clean, and the men we talked with were the soldiers of Spain's new People's Army—disciplined, well-trained, and wise in the knowledge that their country must belong to the people, and not to a handful of generals, counts, and wealthy landowners and industrialists.

These men of Spain's new People's Army know that in the old days nobody cared whether they lived and worked and ate or not; that always they were paid as little as possible; that when they went to vote, their vote counted for nothing so long as the dictator, Primo de Rivero, was in power.

When Primo fell and the people elected a popular democratic government, the fascist elements rose up against them and tried to force them back into political darkness at the point of guns. Nobody cared, either, in the old days whether the people learned to read and write or not. Spain's percentage of illiteracy was enormous.

Now, even in the trenches themselves schools have been set up, and these very soldiers to whom I talked were learning to read and write, and to escape from the darkness of ignorance.

The old days were dark days indeed—and the fascists want those old days back. The soldiers in the trenches of Madrid say, NO! And that is why the fascists do not pass. That is why, for months now, with all the modern implements of warfare, Franco hammers away at the gates of Madrid, but he does not pass. The People's Army says, NO!

When we left the trenches, the sun was sinking in the West over behind the hills which belong to the enemy. With evening, and the coming darkness, the quiet was broken and the crack of rifle and machine-gun fire began to echo through the empty houses. We heard the sharp hiss of bullets above our heads.

Occasionally, a stray shot would hit a wall nearby with a sharp crack. We followed a path back to our car that was more or less out of range of direct fire—but much too near the bullets for a pleasant stroll.

Through the dark and ruined streets of the war zone, back to the equally dark city of Madrid we drove, our headlights dim. And somehow, as I rode through the night now increasingly loud with gun-fire, I kept thinking about the flowers I had seen on the balcony railings of those empty and shell-torn houses.

And I thought that perhaps those flowers might well symbolize the whole struggle in Spain—those flowers blooming so bravely there in the face of fascist fire; those flowers like the brave and beautiful books of Thomas Mann and others that Hitler burned in his bonfire in Berlin:

Those flowers like the brave and hopeful Chinese students the Japanese put before the firing squads in Pekin; those flowers like the young Ethiopians from the hills massacred in Addis Ababa; those flowers like the wonderful old paintings in the museum of the Prado which the fascist shells sought to destroy before they could be carried to safety by the government;

Those flowers like the strong and beautiful working men and women who poured, unarmed, into the streets of Madrid on July 19, and defied the reactionaries in the attempt to seize the city; those flowers blooming in the face of shell fire like the copy-books of the soldiers learning to read and write today in the front-line trenches of Spain.

The fascist guns are turned against the simple words in copy books that for the first time the men of the new army are learning to spell.

The fascists do not like living flowers. That is why the people of

Madrid say, NO—and close their city with a ring of human trenches against the enemy.

The Afro-American, 27 November 1937

N.Y. Nurse Weds Irish Fighter
in Spain's War

By Langston Hughes

Valencia

Miss Salaria Kee of Harlem, charming nurse at one of the American hospitals in Spain, was married on October 2 to John Joseph O'Reilly, ambulance driver from Thurles, County Tipperary, Ireland.

Her husband was one of the first international volunteers to come to fight on the loyalist side in Spain, and was for several months in the trenches. Recently he was transferred to hospital service.

A letter from a fellow-worker in their hospital, written to Joe North, and in turn passed on to Thyra Edwards and myself, gives a graphic description of the wedding of these two internationals from distinct parts of the world mating in Spain. An extract from the letter follows.

"They were married at Villa Paz and the marriage was celebrated with music and dancing. Speeches were made by various American and Spanish guests including the blind soldier, Raven, who spoke for the patients of the hospital, and Dr. Arnold Donawa, member of the staff, who spoke for the hospital.

"Salaria came to Spain in April and has worked at Villa Paz. She is known to hundreds of American boys for her patience, her smile, and her wit. She is a very charming person, and the bridegroom, known as Pat, discovered that as soon as he landed in Villa Paz. He was so much in love with her that he began writing poetry about her, but being a shy Irishman, he was afraid to tell her about it. The other nurses, however, read the poetry and told Salaria.

"Instead of the usual wedding march, a chorus of young Spanish girls sang 'Joven Guardia' and other songs. The old judge from Salices, who sports large handlebar moustaches, performed the ceremony. The three-piece band from Salices supplied the music and it seems to me that although they may not know it, they dished out pretty good swing. The American and Spanish guests gave the bride and bridegroom numerous presents. The affair broke up late, but no one staggered.

"The bride, Salaria, is 26, a graduate of Harlem Hospital, and has been a nurse there. She has also nursed at Sea View Hospital in Staten Island. She is considered by her colleagues to be very efficient and capable. Hemingway and Martha Gellhorn were here October 2, but could not stay for the wedding. They took the story, however.

Other social notes from Spain this week might include the visit of Miss Thyra Edwards of Chicago, the "social" in this case meaning a delegate from the Social Workers' Committee for the Aid of Spanish Democracy. Miss Edwards has just returned to Valencia from Madrid where she was received by the famous loyalist commander, El Campesino, and shown about his headquarters and encampments, where she met various colored officers and soldiers from Cuba who volunteered for service in his ranks.

Miss Edwards is especially interested in the problems of the women and children in war-torn Spain and is bringing back to America a report of her investigations here.

The Afro-American, 11 December 1937

SOLDIERS FROM MANY LANDS
UNITED IN SPANISH FIGHT
Class-Conscious Workers Flock There to Fight
the Same Enemy They Have at Home.

By Langston Hughes

Valencia

They come from all over the world, the members of the International Brigades in Spain. Officially, they say, there are thirty-seven nationalities represented. But I think there are more. All the countries of Europe have sons here in Spain. All the countries of America, too, both the English and Spanish-speaking lands.

Far off Australia is here. China and Japan. Negroes are here from the States, the Islands, Africa. I have seen and talked to them, white, and black, and yellow, and brown. In the trenches, in the cities on leave, wounded in the hospitals. Regiments predominantly English, or predominantly French, or German, understanding and speaking each its own language.

Or individuals scattered in Spanish units, alone in a group that does not know one's tongue or tradition—united only in their anti-fascist ideal: freedom for workers. These are the Internationals! Men who've come from far away of their own free will, to fight in Spain.

Of their own free will. And it is that quality of will which differentiates the international fighters on the side of Spanish democracy from those Germans and Italians and Moors who support the Fascists. In the first place, regular German and Italian soldiers are with Franco because their governments sent them there.

Many of the Germans are professional soldiers, anyway, who fight for a living, like hired gangsters. Many of the Italians are poor peasants whose only way of earning a living wage is in the army—and once there, to blindly obey its orders is their only choice. Abyssinia or Spain as Mussolini chooses, to fight against and kill whom Mussolini chooses.

Even sadder and more ironic than with the others, is the position of the Moors who fight in favor of Fascism. They are illiterate African colonials forced to obey the commands of the Fascist generals in power. To keep up their morale, they are spurred on by promises of loot, rape, and the doubtful pleasure of killing some of those Spaniards who in the past have taken so many shots at them. But unfortunately, the Moors are shooting the wrong way. In pointing their guns against the workers and farmers of democratic Spain, they are only further aiding the rebel generals to tighten more surely their grip of despotism on Africa as well as on Spain.

Germans, Italians, and Moors fighting for Fascism! But on the side of the Spanish government, there are also Germans, Italians, and Moors fighting for a new democracy; economic democracy. A different kind of soldier and a different kind of man. The members of the International Brigades.

In the first place, they know why they are fighting, and that why is made up of very definite reasons. For instance, Germans fighting on the loyalist side in Spain do so because they recognize in Franco the shadow and extension of Hitler and all that Nazism stands for: rigid control of the rights of workers and the suppression of their labor unions; suppression of experimentation in science, and freedom of thought in writing, art, and the theatre, suppression and segregation of racial minorities that happen not to be Nordic, but are instead Jewish or colored.

In other words, Hitler means Jew-baiting, Nordic supremacy, the burning of books and company unions. No decent German likes those things.

Italians are in the International Brigades because they see in Franco the shadow and extension of Mussolini with his cry of eternal war, war, war; his love of oppression in its most savage forms such as the bombing of the helpless natives of Ethiopia and the women and children of Spain; his creation of a land in which all political parties are banned, all workers' organizations are subjected to State control, all books to censorship, and where all male children are taken over by the army as soon as they can walk, to make of them future killers. No decent Italian likes those things.

And so they come to help Spain fight against them, because they know that Franco means a spreading of Fascism and Hitlerism to yet another part of the world. An no good man wishes Fascism to go any further.

As for the Moors who managed to avoid Franco's ranks and instead take up arms for the people's cause—and there are a considerable number—they know that the generals who now control North Africa and support Franco are the same generals who in the old days kept the Moors down by force, sent the Spanish army against them, and shot and starved them into submission.

Now these generals use Moors against the workers and peasants of Spain in order to crush the new bloom of Spanish democracy, deceiving the Moors into believing that it was the workers who oppressed them in the first place. (A very dangerous way, to be sure, of playing with one's colonies—and a way which the common people of England and France had best quickly understand, lest they wake up some morning to find that the ruling class of their own lands also has called in African natives to shoot London or Paris in the back.

In fact, those lands that now talk so much about democracy had better do a little something about it quickly in regard to their colored subjects, lest their colored subjects, confused like the Moors, may not know quite which side to fight on when the struggle comes to a head.)

Fortunately, some Moors and some Africans realize that Fascism can never be, under any guise, a friend of colonial freedom. Those colored colonials who have joined the International Brigades against Franco, understand this.

But colored people are not the only oppressed folks in the world, by any means. From Ireland, that has known oppression for so long, many good fighters have come to republican Spain. Why? Because one of the great enemies of the Spanish people is that same Bank of England that helps starve and exploit Ireland.

France has contributed thousands of men to loyalist Spain, too, because the French workers know that another Fascist border, like Germany's on the edge of France, will so greatly strengthen the Fascist elements within France that no working man will any longer be secure in his right to vote for working class representation in the Chamber of Deputies, if he chooses, or organize a strike for higher wages, or read a book or paper not approved by the wealthy reactionaries that control French finance capital, and that seek to control as well, French men and women, and their labor.

From these countries that I've named and from others all over the world, class-conscious workers come to fight in Spain because they realize that the enemy now firing from the fascist trenches is the same old enemy they have at home—except that at home he still wears a mask, as a rule, whereas in Spain he has not only dropped his mask, but has let his pants down as well.

Give Franco a hood and he would be a member of the Ku Klux Klan, a kleagle. Fascism is what the Ku Klux Klan will be when it combines with the Liberty League and starts using machine guns and airplanes instead of a few yards of rope. Fascism is oppression, terror, and brutality on a big scale.

The colored group must fight it wherever it is found. Opposing it in Spain now as members of the international brigades, are colored men in every branch of the military service, as officers, as soldiers, as scouts, as transport workers, as teachers in the Brigade training schools.

In the Medical Aid as ambulance drivers, one doctor, and a nurse. On a recent visit to the Aragon front I met a dozen men from Harlem, seven colored boys from Los Angeles, a half-dozen from Chicago, and several from my own State of Ohio.

The Afro-American, 18 December 1937

MILT HERNDON DIED TRYING
TO RESCUE WOUNDED PAL:
Brother of Angelo, Leading Machine Gun Section,
Was Liked by All, Hughes Finds.

By Langston Hughes

Valencia

It was quiet on the front. No action. Our attack was over. Silence in the blanket of a rainy night in a valley where perhaps twenty thousand men lie in trenches, behind barricades in ruined villages, squatting beside machine-guns spitting a row of bullets into space. Then, long blanks of silence again.

Afar off, the boom of cannon, steady for maybe half an hour. Perhaps the government guns trained on Zaragossa, as the enemy guns are trained on Madrid. Then silence again. And the rain coming down in a soft, steady drizzle.

Where the tent sags, water drips down and spatters on the table. Two candles burn. Men come in and out with messages for members of the General Staff, papers to sign, calls to the field telephone in a dugout on the side of the hill. The pop of a motorcycle. A courier arriving or departing for the lines.

When the tent flap is lifted, you see the sentry with his gun on his shoulder outside, scarcely visible in the darkness, his capelike coat touching the ground. He stands there silent, on guard in the rain.

Dave Doran comes in, the Political Commisar of the 15th Brigade.

"Sorry," he says, "but we can't go to the Mac-Pap's tonight. Too much rain. Too difficult for you to see the men on a night like this. Besides, his battalion's the furthest away, a couple of miles or more through the trenches, the last in our lines. Instead of your going, I've telephoned for two of the members of Herndon's section to come in and talk to you."

The rain seemed to come down harder than ever. Rain and the dull boom of artillery. It was cold so I went out, and into the next tent to look for an overcoat. One of my tent-mates was spreading down the groundcloth, with a flashlight, preparatory to making our pallets on the damp earth.

"They've just dug a little trench around our tent so the water'll run off," he said. "You know, this is the first night the Estado Mayor's been located here."

"Yes," I said, because I knew that the day before the Fascists had discovered the site of the International's field headquarters and had blasted them with artillery shells, killing three and wounding seven in the bombardment. I'd have been there myself if we hadn't been delayed a day on the road waiting for a truck.

This was my first visit to the Internationals in action. They were on the Aragon front, specifically Fuentes de Ebro—which means the village of Fuentes, located on the River Ebro. The loyalist troops, including the English-speaking battalions of the brigades, had taken Belchite and Quinto a short time before, important victories for the government.

Now our lines lay just outside the town of Fuentes de Ebro. In an attack on Fuentes, Milton Herndon was killed. To learn how Herndon died, I wished to visit the trenches in which his battalion was lying that rainy October night. But my trip had been counter-manded. Instead, two of his comrades were coming to field headquarters behind the lines to talk with me.

I put on my heavy coat and went back to the busy tent to wait. Two or three hours passed. They did not come. Meanwhile, there was a meeting of the Political Commissars from the various International companies, English, American, Irish and Spanish-speaking, on the front.

I was invited to sit in and listen to the problems and daily interests of the men in the trenches whom the Commissars were commis-sioned to look after, to keep in shape physically and mentally.

Nine o'clock came, ten, eleven. Still the men hadn't come from the Mackenzie-Papineau Battalion where Herndon served. The meeting of Commissars broke up. It was raining very hard, so Doran decided to telephone for a truck to carry them back to the trenches where, even then, some of them would have an hour, or two hours' walk to reach their companies.

"Something must have happened that they couldn't leave," Doran said to me regarding the men from the Mac-Pap's. "But I'll phone again and see."

I followed him out into the rain. On our way to the communica-tions dugout, we ran into two men, dark shapes in the dark on the side of the hill.

"Johnson! Sankari!" they said.

·What happened to you?" Doran asked. "We had given you up."

"Snipers must have seen us coming out," one of them answered, "so they kept picking at us all around until we had to stop."

"So many bullets kept whizzing by for a while that we had to lie down in a ditch and stay there more'n an hour."

"Then when we did get out, in the rain, we couldn't find the path up here since you've moved."

But they had finally arrived. Two men from the 4th Company of the Mackenzie-Papineau Battalion who had served under Sergeant Herndon in his machine-gun section. They were big American fellows, standing there in the dark. Dave Doran introduced me: Aaron Johnson of Los Angeles, Hjalmar Sankari of New York.

Back in the candle-lighted tent, I saw that one was a colored boy, dark-brown skin, young—Johnson. And the other was a Scandinavian-American, blond, light-skinned, and strong.

"You'd better go back in the truck I'm sending for," Dave Doran advised them as he started out to phone, "so there won't be much time to talk."

The two men wiped the rain from their faces and we sat down on a bank of earth that had been dug out like a hollow square around the table. The others left us alone in the tent. I began to ask questions about Herndon and his life in Spain but, at first, it was a rather halting interview. No fighter likes to talk much about a comrade who's just been killed. But these men were his friends. They had come to tell me about him.

"Milt Herndon! He died like this," they said. Sometimes one talked, sometimes the other. One answered a question, another added a phrase. Two voices in the night, a colored voice and a white voice. Two American voices telling how Milton Herndon died.

"He died like this," they said. "He was taking the second machine-gun over the top. He was the sergeant, the section leader. He had three guns under him. He was taking the second gun over the top with his men. We went about three hundred meters up a little rise— when all of a sudden the Fascists opened up on us. We had to stop. A regular rain of bullets.

·"They got one of our comrades, Irving, and he fell just ahead of us on top of the ridge in full view of the Fascist fire. He was wounded in the leg and couldn't move. The man nearest to him, Smitty, raised up to drag him back aways, and a bullet got Smitty in the heart. Got him right in the heart. Then Herndon crawled on up the slope to rescue the wounded boy. They got Herndon, too.

"Through the head, through the mouth—two bullets, just like that! And Herndon and Smitty both died. The other boy lived. He's in the hospital now. But Herndon and Smitty were killed right there. It was October thirteenth our first day in the lines. At one o'clock we went over the top."

The rain came down in torrents on the little tent where we were sitting. A motor truck drew up outside. We heard the fellows piling in for their return to the trenches. Someone came to say that they would wait for us to finish our conversation. But I did not like to keep a whole truck full of men standing in the rain.

"Tell me a little of what he was like," I said, "before you go. I know Angelo, but I never knew Milton."

"He used to talk a lot about Angelo," Sankari said. "He was proud of his brother. But Milton was smart, too, and he knew what lies behind this war. He was always politically alert. He worked hard in the company and in his section. The men liked him. He had both Americans and English under him, and we all liked him."

"Two of us are colored in the company besides Herndon," Johnson said. "Myself and Charlie Lewis from New York. We all liked Herndon. He worked hard. He was good natured. He was a good card player, too. A good fellow."

"He wanted to be a dynamiter," the Scandinavian added. "He was a big tall fellow, used to be a miner, and he would have been in one of the Spanish companies as a dynamiter if he could've spoken Spanish. He was a good singer, too. Everybody liked him."

"He and Smitty were both fine fellows," Johnson said. "They were good friends, too. Smitty was white. They're buried together."

"Out in No-Man's Land by Fuentes, we buried them that night," Sankari said.

"You know, our machine-gun company was named after Frederick Douglass," Johnson added as they left the tent. "Herndon suggested the name, and when we named it the Frederick Douglass Machine-Gun Company, he made a speech on the connections between our rights at home in America and the fight here in Spain. He said, 'Yesterday, Ethiopia. Today, Spain. Tomorrow, maybe America. Fascism won't stop anywhere—until we stop it.' That's what he said."

The truck rumbled away in the blackness of the downpour, its headlights out. With it went the two young Americans, one dark with the blood of Africa, and the other light-haired and Scandinavian. Together they had come an hour earlier through the rain, stooping in the trenches, hiding in roadside ditches away from the bullets, in order to tell me how two others, Americans, one black and one white, had died to stop Fascism. And how, at the moment of their death, they saved a wounded comrade from the bullets.

I remembered long ago it was written, "Greater love hath no man than this, that he lay down his life for another." And I thought how Milton Herndon had died not only to save another comrade, or another country, Spain, but for all of us in America, as well. You see, he understood the connections between the enemy at home and the enemy in Spain: They are the same enemy.

The Afro-American, 1 January 1938

FIGHTERS FROM OTHER LANDS LOOK TO OHIO MAN FOR FOOD:
Abraham Lewis, as Quartermaster in Spain, Also Attends to Clothing and Recreational Needs

By Langston Hughes

Valencia

He was about to start out with two trucks, several helpers, and several thousand pesetas on a food purchasing tour for the various kitchens at the Anglo-American Training Base of the International Brigades in the heart of Spain. He was a heavy-set, dark brownskin fellow of perhaps 35, snappy and efficient-looking in his well-kept officer's uniform.

He had little time to talk to me, as the trucks were about to get under way, but while the chauffeurs were getting their gas for the journey, he told me something of himself and his work in Spain.

Abraham Lewis is his name. He comes from Cleveland, Ohio, where he was one of the most active workers in the Future Outlook League, a leading colored organization there. He has been in Spain almost a year. At first he was attached to a transport regiment and after two months of service he was made a sergeant.

Now he is a lieutenant, and the quartermaster in charge at the English-speaking training base with a large staff of various nationalities under him, American, English, and Spanish. His responsibilities include the feeding, clothing, sanitary, and recreational facilities of the entire base. No small job for one man.

Abraham Lewis, however, is not without experience in such work. He was formerly a steward on an American government boat and there aquired the knowledge of handling food and preparing menus. Here in Spain, though, the feeding of Internationals is no simple problem. In the first place, the Spaniards cook with olive oil, a procedure not agreeable to the palate of most foreigners.

Lewis had to find various available substitutes for this oil, substitutes that would appeal to the International mouths at his tables in a land where lard and butter are not easily to be gotten. Then there was the problem of cooks. Very few of the International Brigaders who came to Spain wanted to serve as cooks. They wanted to fight.

So Lewis had to train Spanish cooks in American ways of cooking, stressing as well sanitation and efficiency, especially in the matter of time—having food ready exactly at the hour when it should be served.

For Lewis who speaks little Spanish, this has been a double task. He has, of course, an interpreter. But because many of his Spanish kitchen workers could neither read nor write, written orders and listed menus were at first impossible.

Out of twenty-seven cooks and helpers, only seven were literate. So Lewis organized classes for them. Now, after five months, seventeen have learned to read their own language, Spanish. For this achievement the U.G.T. Trade Unions, to which the kitchen employees belong, have complimented Lewis in an official letter.

But Lewis's job includes much more than food. As Quartermaster, he is in charge of all distribution of clothing and bedding at the camp, and has installed a modern American filing system to keep track of things. He has set up a tailoring repair service, employing women of the village. He has modernized greatly the camp laundry.

He has set up a shoe-repair shop which was badly needed, but lacking before Lewis came. At present, through the various services of which Lewis is in charge, more than a hundred thousand pesetas a month pass through his hands for purchases and expenses.

Abraham Lewis is deeply interested in and proud of his job. He is proud of the opportunity which the International Brigades have given him to make use of his full capacities for organizational and administrative work. He knows that in America such opportunities come too seldom to members of the darker race. Here he has done well in the responsible position which he occupies.

Just before the trucks returned to staff headquarters to pick him up for their buying expedition, I asked Lewis what he thought of Spain and the Spanish people. His answer was an enthusiastic one, and a very racial one. He said, "Here nobody sneers at a colored person because he has a position of authority. Everybody tries to help him. Everybody salutes him.

"A colored person has a chance to develop here. Spain is all right! And in the International Brigades, people of all races, even if they can't speak your language, help you and work with you. That's the kind of comradeship that gets things done!"

The trucks came, and he was notified that they were waiting. Lewis shook my hand warmly and went away. It was midnight. At dawn they would be in the distant city where the wholesale houses and supply bases were. With him on the first truck were two white helpers. On the second truck also, his co-workers were white.

When will we learn to work together like that in America? I wondered. In Spain now the Internationals of all races stand against Fascism and its barbarous theories of white supremacy and working-class oppression. When the black and white workers of America learn to stand together in the same fashion, no oppressive forces in the world can hurt them.

When Abraham Lewis comes home, he can no doubt help America achieve that unity. That is what I thought as I watched his trucks drive away through the Spanish night across La Mancha where centuries ago Don Quixote wandered with his lance.

The Afro-American, 8 January 1938

PITTSBURGH SOLDIER HERO,.
BUT TOO BASHFUL TO TALK:
Cited by Spanish Loyalists for Bravery in
Mopping Up—Italian Prisoner Maybe
Thought About Ethiopia

By Langston Hughes

Valencia

We sat in the improvised office of the daily mimeographed bulletin of the Washington-Lincoln Battalion in the middle of the ruined city of Quinto shortly after the loyalist forces took it away from the Fascists.

Artillery and air-bombs had left few buildings standing whole. The Brigade library, post-office, and bulletin had taken possession of one of the more or less whole houses left standing. Ralph Thornton was acting as a clerk there when I saw him.

We sat in the sunlight near the door, and I tried to get him to tell me why he had just been cited for bravery beyond the ordinary call of duty, and why the brigade had presented him a gold watch.

Thornton, light-brown skin fellow from the smoky city of Pittsburgh, was loathe to talk about himself. "Oh, it wasn't much," he insisted. "We just took four prisoners in Belchite; that's all. Me and two other boys captured them."

Luckily, two other members of Thornton's outfit were sitting there with us. They weren't at all bashful in talking about Thornton, even if he wouldn't talk much about himself.

The story was that at the taking of Belchite by the Spanish People's Army including the American units of the International Brigades, one of the largest buildings in the city, filled with Fascists, held out even after our troops had entered the town.

At dawn a group of Internationals were ordered to take it. Ralph Thornton was in that group. They stormed the building with hand grenades and took it for the government in the face of heavy resistance.

That same morning, Thornton and two white comrades, Ben Findley and Carl Geiser, were given several blocks of houses to inspect in the captured city. Many of the houses were in ruins, but some stood intact. From upper windows, snipers still operated.

Behind barred doors and closed blinds Fascists who had been unable to escape crouched in hiding. Inspecting these ominously quiet houses was no gentle task. You could easily get a hand grenade in the face.

They went up the narrow stone stairs of an ancient old house with walls three feet thick. Dark cold silence everywhere. But on the top floor, the third, when Thornton opened the door to the front bedroom, the silence was suddenly perfumed with the scent of powder and acrid smoke stung him in the eyes and burned his throat.

Someone moved in the dark, turned and cried out, then jumped to his feet crying, "Salud!" At the same time he threw a rifle from him. The gun was still hot when Thornton picked it up.

The man was a Fascist who had been lying there sniping on the government soldiers. Now he cowered in a corner crying "Salud!" The word with which the loyalists greet one another. But he didn't look like a man who would say "Salud," naturally.

The captured sniper turned out to be the vice president of the local Falangists, the town's Fascists organization (like our Ku Klux Klan) and one of the most active enemies of republicanism in that secion of Aragon.

Further inspection revealed several cupboards in the house filled with gold and hidden jewels.

Nearby, in another house whose inhabitants had been unable to flee, the three Americans found an old woman sitting at a window. They asked her whether there was anyone hiding in the house. She said, "No."

A careful search of the premises revealed a hidden opening leading to a tunnel dug beneath the dwelling. Down there in the dark, at the end of the tunnel, an Italian soldier was hiding—one of Mussolini's contributions to the conquering of Spain.

He probably thought he was in Ethiopia by mistake when he saw Thornton's dark face inviting him to come out and surrender.

Before they went back to staff headquarters that morning, Thornton and his comrades had taken two other Fascist prisoners and had made sure that there were no more snipers in the blocks of houses they had been sent out to inspect.

Because of Thornton's valor at Belchite, his part in the storming of the Fascist-held building, and the importance of the prisoners he took, the whole brigade united in the presentation of a watch to him on the day when his citation for bravery arrived.

No doubt Thornton was pleased, but he was too modest to talk about it to a writer.

Thornton says he used to be a newsboy in Pittsburgh. And more recently he worked for the Center Printing Company. He says the skies of Spain are the most beautiful he's ever seen—after Pittsburgh—but that there's too much olive oil in the cooking. When the war is over, he's coming home.

The Afro-American, 15 January 1938

Walter Cobb, Driving Captured Fascist Truck, Mistaken by Own Men for Moor, but Language Saves Him

By Langston Hughes

Barcelona

The first time I met Walter Cobb was in the Puerta del Sol, that big and busy square that is the heart of Madrid. An American in town on leave and I were looking for a place to have luncheon. Across the square came three internationals in their uniforms, two of them white and one colored.

The colored fellow had his pack on his back and his rifle on his shoulder, fully equipped to do battle. The three of them were talking French in the heat of a summer afternoon.

"That must be a French West African," I said to the fellow with me.

"No, it isn't either," he answered. "That's Walter Cobb."

And Walter Cobb it was, from St. Louis. He happened at that time to be the only American with an all-French Battallion. How he got there I was never able to find out, but there he was.

The next time I saw Cobb, it was three months later on the Aragon front. In the fall he had been transferred to an American brigade, one of the transport units, and this time he was talking Spanish to a girl who worked at the camp kitchen!

"I have to keep in practice with my languages," he explained. "Why, if I hadn't known Spanish, a week or so ago here, they would've taken me for a Moor, and made me a prisoner, sure."

"Who, our own soldiers?" I asked.

"Right! You see, I was driving a captured Fascist truck that we took at Belchite. I was bringing it back behind the lines to be repaired, and we hadn't had a chance yet to paint out the Fascist markings on it. It was night, and in the dark between a place called Todo and El Varade some Spanish soldiers on control-duty stopped me at the cross-roads and threw their flashlights on the truck.

"When they saw me, colored as I am, and saw that truck with the Fascist signs on it, they thought sure I was a Moor who had got lost and had accidentally run across the line somewhere. They yelled at me to come down, and held their guns on me until I got off the truck. But by that time, they saw that I was an international, and when I showed them my papers and told them we had captured that big truck from the Fascists, and that it belonged to our side now, they almost hugged me!

"But suppose I hadn't been able to speak a little Spanish and explain what I was doing driving a Fascist truck in Loyalist territory so near the front!"

Then Cobb went on to tell me that in the smaller villages, being quite dark in color, he is often the center of an interested and friendly crowd. In the cities of Spain, a dark person attracts no attention, but in some of the smaller towns they may never have seen a real colored man before.

Their curiosity, however, is always friendly, and village families often vie with one another in offers of hospitality should their colored visitor wish to eat a meal or spend a night there.

Walter Cobb has been in Spain for eight months. At first in the infantry on the mountainous Guadarrama front with a French company, now he is back with the Americans again where the laughter of this young and jolly boy from St. Louis helps to keep his whole regiment in good humor.

The Afro-American, 22 January 1938

HOWARD MAN FIGHTING AS SPANISH LOYALIST:
Thaddeus Battle Asserts Students Should
Oppose Fascist Rise in World

By Langston Hughes

When the 1st Regiment de Train of the 15th Brigade was at rest not far from Madrid last fall, its camp was near a road. The tents were so cleverly camouflaged (painted a zig-zag green and brown), and so carefully hidden under trees that, from the highway, it was difficult to know there was a camp there.

Once the enemy bombers came over and dropped a few bombs, but they landed in the woods and did no damage. The Madrid front, a few kilometers away, was not dangerously near, but still near enough for the wind to bring with it the sound of heavy artillery and exploding mines. The first day I visited the camp, there was a steady rumble in the air.

Thaddeus Battle, one of the two colored members of the regiment, was a student at Howard University. He intended to major in political science before he came to Spain, and will resume his studies in Washington when he returns.

He is a mild-mannered, quiet young man, wears glasses, and busies himself studying Spanish and French during his spare time when the regiment is not in service, or the Fascist planes are not zooming overhead.

Battle came originally from North Carolina. At Howard he was on the freshman football team. His main off-campus activity was helping with the Washington work of the National Negro Congress. And he was very happy to read in copies of the *Afro-American* that reached Madrid, about the successful Philadelphia meeting of the congress in October. He wondered if there were many colored students taking part in the sessions.

"Our students must take a more active interest in labor problems, in the efforts of colored workers to better their conditions," Battle said as we sat smoking in his tent one chilly autumn afternoon.

"At home in America the forces of reaction can so easily use colored workers as a decoy to keep labor from achieving unity. That makes it easier for them to bring about a regime of repression in real Fascist style at home."

"Can colored college students help prevent this?" I asked.

"Of course they can," Battle replied. "Student movements in America are beginning to carry some weight as a serious force in our national life.

"Colored students must be a part of these movements whenever they are directed against the spread of reactionary tendencies, against war, and toward the strengthening of real democracy. I mean economic as well as political democracy!"

Outside we heard what seemed to be the hum of planes. We stuck our heads out of the tent and looked up, but nothing was in sight, so we went on with our conversation.

"Colored college students must realize, too, the connection between the international situation and our problems at home," Battle continued.

"When we see certain things happening in Europe and Asia that may involve America in another world war, then, and only then do we see clearly the need for combating such tendencies at home and abroad.

"Right here in Madrid I've seen how Fascists destroy schools and libraries. University City, a million-dollar educational center, is in ruins!

"Why gain culture only to see it destroyed? Franco destroys what it has taken people years to build. He burns books and closes schools and stifles education.

"In America our students, colored and white, must take a stand against all factors that even point toward a Fascist type of social order. And our colored campuses should play a much more vital role in national, and even international affairs, than they have done in the past."

I agreed with Battle, and made notes of what he said.

We talked until the big gong for supper sounded and we went to get in line before the cook tent. Three Spanish women were ladling out a delicious rabbit stew.

The long line of men forming there were a typical section of the English-speaking units of the International Brigades in Spain. There were Irish lads, English and American Jews, a Southern father and son from Oklahoma, two cousins from a wealthy old family in California, an Australian school teacher, and two colored men.

One was Bernard Rucker, a worker from Columbus, O., the other

Thaddeus Battle of Howard University, taking time out from books to learn from life.

The Afro-American, 5 February 1938

HARLEM BALL PLAYER NOW CAPTAIN IN SPAIN:
Basilio Cueria, Head of Machine Gun Company Called One of the Best Officers

By Langston Hughes

Basilio Cueria, well-known colored Cuban baseball player and resident of Harlem is now the captain of a machine gun company in loyalist Spain. More than a year ago, Cueria went to Spain to enlist in the International Brigades.

For five months he was with the Lincoln Battalion on the Jarrama front during the hardest of the battles there, holding off the Italian and Moorish troops of Franco's Fascist legions who sought to enter Madrid.

At present Cueria is with an all Spanish brigade under the leadership of the famous peasant general, "El Campesino." While this brigade was training new recruits at Alcalá de Henares, ancient birthplace of Cervantes, I often visited them and talked frequently with the tall fine looking young captain who was immensely popular with the officers and men under his command.

Campesino himself told me that Cueria was one of the best of the officers in his brigade, the 1st Shock Brigade, 4th Battalion, 46th Division of the Spanish People's Army. Even when General Miaja, heroic defender of Madrid and member of the Spanish general staff, inspected the Campesino troops, Cueria and his company were singled out for special attention.

On the field, they gave a lightning demonstration of how quickly a machine gun may be assembled. Cueria and his men put their machine guns together with such rapidity, from the various parts which each man carries, that they were declared a model unit.

Back home in America, old baseball fans often speak of Cueria. A baseball player in Havana before he moved to the United States ten years ago, Cueria has long been associated with the game. He was a catcher with the Cuban Stars. Then in 1929 he became manager of the Miami Red Sox. And later he was with the Cuban Giants.

He has also played with a number of other clubs, and in New York he formed the Julio Antonio Mella Baseball Club in the Latin-American section of Harlem. Cueria is now interested in developing baseball as a recreational sport for the Spanish soldiers.

A year in Spain, and Cueria is already a veteran of many battles. In the early days, the Jarrama front was one of the most active in Spain. Transferred from there, Cueria took part in the great battles at Quijorna and Brunete last spring. For days he was under one of the most terrific artillery and air bombardments known in history.

At Brunete, near Madrid, the rebels put into action the largest air force yet used in modern warfare up to that time. Trenches, troop concentrations, convoys, roads, all were bombed hour after hour, day after day. From Brunete the government was forced to retreat, leaving a ruined city that Fascist explosives had destroyed.

Today Brunete is no-man's land, the government lines being just outside the town. But the offensive gained important objectives for the government, including the town of Quijorna, and Cueria came through it all unscathed. Now his division is reported in action at Teruel.

Captain Cueria says that his men are fine fellows to lead, and that all of them are proud to be fighting under Campesino, who is a worker-peasant commander right up from the ranks of the people. Campesino is indeed Spain's most colorful military man and in a year and a half of warfare has become almost a folk hero.

The people say that he rides into battle with his men, often mounted on a tank in full view of the enemy. And another story is that once badly wounded, he was carried behind the lines to a dressing station where his wounds were given emergency bandaging and placed in an ambulance to be rushed to a hospital at the rear. The ambulance started off. But the next thing the attendant knew was that there was no Campesino. He had opened the door, stepped out, and was shortly back in the midst of the battle with his men, bandages and all.

The soldiers laugh at him and love him, and follow him without question, so I could easily believe Cueria when he told me that everybody wants to fight with Campesino.

Since there are a large number of Cubans fighting in Spain on the government side, many of them colored Cubans, I asked Cueria how they were received, and whether any of them had ever been taken for Moors, or had encountered any color prejudice. Cueria laughed and said that sometimes dark Cubans were asked by Spaniards whether they were Moorish, but never in an unfriendly way, since the Spaniards have no color feeling about the Moors. (And there are Moors on the loyal side, as well as with Franco.)

But toward Cubans, who are a Spanish speaking people themselves, Spain has always been most hospitable. Before the revolt many Cubans lived in Spain.

And Cubans, of color especially, who sought another homeland often preferred Spain to the United States where they might run into difficulties on the basis of complexion. But Cueria himself assured me that he liked Harlem and would be coming back to America when the war is over. His family is in New York.

"Our side is sure to win," he said. "We can't let the Fascists put it over on us. They'd put all the worst old prejudices back in to force and probably even introduce new ones, like Hitler and his Aryanism in Germany. No, we're not going to let them win!"

"Anything else you'd like to say to the folks back home?" I asked as I said goodbye just before the Teruel offensive.

"Well, tell all the baseball players hello for me," Cueria said. "And tell the Mella Club to keep up that team in Harlem, so I can play with them when I get back. Tell all those Harlem baseball players hello!"

The Afro-American, 12 February 1938

AFRO WRITER NICKED BY BULLET IN SPAIN:
Langston Hughes, Hurt, Back in U.S.
After Six Months With Loyalists

New York

Colored people who travel in Europe are beginning to realize more and more what is meant by Fascism, as they note a rising color bar that blocks them in many places where they were formerly greeted with generous enthusiasm.

This was the view expressed by Langston Hughes, poet, playwright and novelist, who arrived in this country Wednesday on the Cunarder, Berengaría, after six months in Spain, where he wrote exclusive stories of the Spanish war for the *Afro-American* newspapers.

Hughes brought back one physical souvenir of his experiences in Spain, in the shape of a bullet wound in his left elbow. A dum dum bullet nicked him while he was peering through a sight in Madrid at the enemy lines about 100 yards away. The editor of the Madrid Sun, who was standing nearby, was also hit.

"The Fascist ideal is nordic," Hughes said, and includes an intense subjugation of colonial peoples. Colored people in this country and any place in the world, by and large, are treated as inferiors by Fascist nations. Italy and Germany, the two nations who have enabled General Franco to control half of Spain, represent the Fascistic forces that are propagating in every way possible the ideal of racial separatism and the inferiority of darker peoples.

"If these countries can gain control in Spain, a country which has never known color prejudice, they will not only implant color prejudice, but enable the Fascist forces in America to take new courage in their ceaseless drive to oppress colored people in this country."

Hughes pointed out that a colored musician in Germany was recently expelled because he lived in the home of a white woman. This, he added, would never have been considered three or four years ago.

Because 90 per cent of the darker peoples in the world, including colored people in America, are workers, and poor people, when it is realized that Fascism is definitely an ideology which tends to limit the advance of any working people, whether white or black, and to abolish any type of labor union, it can be easily seen why colored people everywhere should fight it, he said.

"Spain is only a week's journey from New York," he said, "less than half an hour by cable, and a split second by radio. The rebel general, Franco, can even now address American audiences on short wave radio, and pour his anti-Negro, anti-labor poison into American minds."

Praising the kindness and total lack of color prejudice in the Spanish people, Hughes said:

"They greet the music of Cab Calloway, Duke Ellington, and other orchestra leaders with the applause of seeing old familiars who have made good. They love Marian Anderson.

"Our musicians, concert artists and stage stars have represented our people admirably abroad. It is unfortunate, though, that American movies, which are popular in Spain as elsewhere on the continent, have shown colored actors only in the role of buffoon or servant.

"This makes the Spanish people wonder why a personage like Marian Anderson does not appear the star of some movie story."

Hughes lectured in Madrid, spoke regularly about twice a week over the short wave radio on an international hookup in that country, and made a record of one of them in Paris.

He had dinner with General Miaja, leader of the Loyalist forces, was the guest of honor at a dinner last November together with Ernest Hemingway, the novelist, at a celebration of the first year of the successful defense of Madrid. The dinner was sponsored by the American Battalion in Spain.

"Spanish newspapers," despite the fact that they write mostly about the war, take time out to tell of the Scottsboro case," he said, "and the marriage of Josephine Baker was given considerable publicity there."

Hughes, who speaks excellent Spanish, translated some of the works of García Lorca, greatest modern Spanish poet, who was killed in the war last July. He expects to translate a poem he wrote called "King of Harlem," the only poem dealing with the American Negro by this Spanish poet.

Traveling back to America by way of Barcelona, and Paris, Hughes said, Adelaide Hall, the night club star, has opened her new night spot, "The Big Apple," one of the smartest clubs in the French metropolis. In Paris he attended a Christmas ball at Epinay, a suburb of Paris, in the City Hall. The deputy mayor, Felix Merim, and his French wife, presided over the affair. He found a hotel in the heart of Montmarte, operated by Ethiopians and filled with Ethiopian refugees.

In Paris his "Ways of White Folks," and his play, "Troubled Island," having to do with Haiti, are being translated for publication in French.

Terming the Spanish people so amazingly kind that they "even tell you to come back later, if they have no change when you make a purchase," Hughes concluded:

"Madrid is the most thrilling and poetic city in the world. It is an heroic place."

Hughes will spend about ten days in New York before going on to Montreal, Canada, where he will give a lecture on Spain.

"After that," he added, "there are so many things to work out that I cannot say just what I'll be doing, or where I'll be doing it."

The Afro-American, 29 January 1938

II. POETRY

Air Raid: Barcelona

Black smoke of sound
Curls against the midnight sky.

Deeper than a whistle,
Louder than a cry,
Worse than a scream
Tangled in the wail
Of a nightmare dream,
     The siren
Of the air raid sounds.

Flames and bombs and
Death in the ear!
The siren announces
Planes drawing near.
Down from bedrooms
Stumble women in gowns.
Men, half-dressed,
Carrying children rush down.
Up in the sky-lanes
Against the stars
A flock of death birds
Whose wings are steel bars
Fill the sky with a low dull roar
Of a plane,
     two planes,
          three planes,
                    five planes,
                    or more.
The anti-aircraft guns bark into space.
The searchlights make wounds
On the night's dark face.
The siren's wild cry
Like a hollow scream
Echoes out of hell in a nightmare dream.
     Then the BOMBS fall!

All other noises are nothing at all
        When the first BOMBS fall.
All other noises ae suddenly still
        When the BOMBS fall.
All other noises are deathly still
As blood spatters the wall
And the whirling sound
Of the iron star of death
Comes hurtling down.
No other noises can be heard
As a child's life goes up
In the night like a bird.
Swift pursuit planes
Dart over the town,
Steel bullets fly
Slitting the starry silk
        Of the sky:
A bomber's brought down
In flames orange and blue,
And the night's all red
Like blood, too.
        The last BOMB falls.

The death birds wheel East
To their lairs again
Leaving iron eggs
In the streets of Spain.
With wings like black cubes
Against the far dawn,
The stench of their passage
Remains when they're gone.
In what was a courtyard
A child weeps alone.

Men uncover bodies
From ruins of stone.

From: *Esquire* 10 (October 1938):40.

From Spain to Alabama

Where have the people gone
That they do not sing
Their flamencos?

> The people
> Have gone nowhere:
> They still sing
> Their flamencos.

Where have the people gone
That they do not sing
Their blues?

> The people
> Have gone nowhere:
> They still sing
> Their blues

From: *Experiment*, Summer, 1949, p. 276.

Hero—International Brigade

Blood,
Or a flag,
Or a flame
Or life itself
Are they the same:
Our dream?
    I came.
An ocean in-between
And half a continent.
Frontiers,
And mountains skyline tall,
And governments that told me NO,
YOU CANNOT GO!
    I came.
On tomorrow's bright frontiers
I placed the strength and wisdom
Of my years.
Not much,
For I am young.
(*Was* young,
Perhaps it's better said—
For now I'm dead.)

But had I lived four score and ten
Life could not've had
A better end.
I've given what I wished
And what I had to give
That others live.
And when the bullets
Cut my heart away,
And the blood
Gushed to my throat
I wondered if it were blood
Gushing there.
Or a red flame?

Or just my death
Turned into life?
They're all the same:
Our dream!
  My death!
  Your life!
  Our blood!
  One flame!
They're all the same!

From: *The Heart of Spain*, ed. Alvah Bessie, (New York: Veterans of the Abraham Lincoln Brigade Inc., 1952), pp. 325-26.

Letter From Spain
Addressed To Alabama

                                        Lincoln Battalion,
                                        International Brigades,
                                        November Something, 1937.
Dear Brother at home:

We captured a wounded Moor today.
He was just as dark as me.
I said, Boy, what you been doin' here
Fightin' against the free?

He answered something in a language
I couldn't understand.
But somebody told me he was sayin'
They nabbed him in his land

And made him join the fascist army
And come across to Spain.
And he said he had a feelin'
He'd never get back home again.

He said he had a feelin'
This whole thing wasn't right.
He said he didn't know
The folks he had to fight.

And as he lay there dying
In a village we had taken,
I looked across to Africa
And seed foundations shakin'.

Cause if a free Spain wins this war,

The colonies, too, are free—
Then something wonderful'll happen
To them Moors as dark as me.

I said, I guess that's why old England
And I reckon Italy, too,
Is afraid to let a workers' Spain
Be too good to me and you—

Cause they got slaves in Africa—
And they don't want' em to be free.
Listen, Moorish prisoner, hell!
Here, shake hands with me!

I knelt down there beside him,
And I took his hand—
But the wounded Moor was dyin'
And he didn't understand.

Salud,

Johnny

From: *The Volunteer for Liberty*, November 15, 1937, p. 3)

Moonlight in Valencia: Civil War

Moonlight in Valencia:
The moon meant planes.
The planes meant death.
And not heroic death.
Like death on a poster:
An officer in a pretty uniform
Or a nurse in a clean white dress—
But death with steel in your brain,
Powder burns on your face,
Blood spilling from your entrails,
And you didn't laugh
Because there was no laughter in it.
You didn't cry PROPAGANDA either.
The propaganda was too much
For everybody concerned.
It hurt you to your guts.
It was real
As anything you ever saw
In the movies:
Moonlight . . .
Me caigo en la ostia!
Bombers over
Valencia.

From *Seven Poets in Search of an Answer*, ed. Thomas Yoseloff (New York, Bernard Ackerman, 1944), p. 51.

Madrid—1937

Damaged by shells, many of the clocks on the public buildings in
Madrid have stopped. At night, the streets are pitch dark.

—News Item

Put out the lights and stop the clocks.
Let time stand still,
Again man mocks himself
And all his human will to build and grow.
　　Madrid!
The fact and symbol of man's woe.
　　Madrid!
Time's end and throw-back,
Birth of darkness,
Years of light reduced:
The ever minus of the brute,
The nothingness of barren land
And stone and metal,
Emptiness of gold,
The dullness of a bill of sale:
BOUGHT AND PAID FOR! SOLD!
Stupidity of hours that do not move
Because all clocks are stopped.
Blackness of nights that do not see
Because all lights are out.
　　Madrid!
Beneath the bullets!
　　Madrid!
Beneath the bombing planes!
　　Madrid!
In the fearful dark!

Oh, mind of man!
So long to make a light

Of fire,
    of oil,
        of gas,
And now electric rays.
So long to make a clock
Of sun-dial,
    sand-dial,
        figures,
And now two hands that mark the hours.
Oh, mind of man!
So long to struggle upward out of darkness
To a measurement of time—
And now:
These guns,
These brainless killers in the Guadarrama hills
Trained on Madrid
To stop the clocks in the towers
And shatter all their faces
Into a million bits of nothingness
In the city
That will not bow its head
To darkness and to greed again:
That dares to dream a cleaner dream!
Oh, mind of man
Moulded into a metal shell—
Left-overs of the past
That rain dull hell and misery
On the world again—
Have your way
And stop the clocks!
Bomb out the lights!
And mock yourself!
Mock all the rights of those
Who live like decent folk.
Let guns alone salute
The wisdom of our age
With dusty powder marks
On yet another page of history.
Let there be no sense of time,

Nor measurement of light and dark,
In fact, no light at all!
Let mankind fall
Into the deepest pit that ignorance can dig
For us all!
Descent is quick.
To rise again is slow.
In the darkness of her broken clocks
Madrid cries NO!
In the timeless midnight of the Fascist guns,
Madrid cries NO!
To all the killers of man's dreams,
Madrid cries NO!

    To break that NO apart
    Will be to break the human heart.
               Madrid, 24 September 1937.

Unpublished poem. Inscribed: "To Arthur Spingarn, Sincerely, Langston."
The Arthur B. Spingarn Papers, Moorland-Spingarn Collection,
Howard University Library.

Song of Spain

Come now, all you who are singers,
And sing me the song of Spain.
Sing it very simply that I might understand.

What is the song of Spain?

Flamenco is the song of Spain:
Gypsies, guitars, dancing
Death and love and heartbreak
To a heel tap and a swirl of fingers
On three strings.
Flamenco is the song of Spain.

I do not understand.

Toros are the song of Spain:
The bellowing bull, the red cape,
A sword thrust, a horn tip,
The torn suit of satin and gold,
Blood on the sand
Is the song of Spain.

I do not understand.

Pintura is the song of Spain:
Goya, Velasquez, Murillo,
Splash of color on canvass,
Whirl of cherub-faces.
La Maja Desnuda's
The song of Spain.

What's that?

Don Quixote! España!
Aquel rincón de la Mancha de
Cuyo nombre no quiero acordarme. . . .

That's the song of Spain.

    You wouldn't kid me, would you?
    A bombing plane's
    The song of Spain.
    Bullets like rain's
    The song of Spain.
    Poison gas is Spain.
    A knife in the back
    And its terror and pain is Spain.

Toros, flamenco, paintings, books—

    Not Spain.

The people are Spain:
The people beneath that bombing plane
With its wings of gold for which I pay—
I, a worker, letting my labor pile
Up millions for bombs to kill a child—
I bought those bombs for Spain!
Workers made those bombs for a Fascist Spain!
Will I make them again, and yet again?
    Storm clouds move fast.
    Our sky is gray.
    The white devils of the terror
    Await their day
When bombs'll fall not only on Spain—
    But on me and you!

Workers, make no bombs again!
Workers, mine no gold again!
Workers, lift no hand again
To build up profits for the rape of Spain!
Workers, see yourselves as Spain!
Workers, know that we too can cry.
Lift arms in vain, run, hide, die:
    Too late!
    The bombing plane!

Workers, make no bombs again
Except that they be made for us
   To hold and guard
Lest some Franco steal into our backyard
Under the guise of a patriot
Waving a flag and mouthing rot
And dropping bombs from a Christian steeple
   On the people.

   I made those bombs for Spain.
   I must not do it again.
   I made those bombing planes.
   I must not do it again.

   I made rich the grandees and lords
   Who hire Franco to lead his gang-hordes
   Against Spain.

   I must never do that again.

I must drive the bombers out of Spain!
I must drive the bombers out of the world!
I must take the world for my own again—

   A worker's world
   Is the song of Spain.

From: Langston Hughes, *A New Song* (New York: International Workers
   Order, 1938), pp. 20-23.

Tomorrow's Seed

Proud banners of death,
I see them waving
There against the sky,
Struck deep in Spanish earth
Where your dark bodies lie
Inert and helpless—
So they think
Who do not know
That from your death
New life will grow.
For there are those who cannot see
The mighty roots of liberty
Push upward in the dark
To burst in flame—
A million stars—
And one your name:
     Man
Who fell in Spanish earth:
Human seed
For freedom's birth.

From: *The Heart of Spain,* ed. Alvah Bessie, (New York: Veterans of the Abraham Lincoln Brigade Inc., 1952), p. 325.

III. ¿QUIÉN ES LANGSTON HUGHES?

Presentación de Langston Hughes

José Antonio Fernández de Castro

Carl Van Vechten, notable novelista norteamericano, al presentar (1925) al público de su patria a Langston Hughes—joven poeta negro que acaba de visitarnos—decía: "Seguro que el relato completo de esa correría fantásticamente deliciosa—que es la vida de L. H.— resultará la más fascinadora novela picaresca." Y en efecto, antes de cumplir doce años—nació en Joplin, Missouri, en 1901—L.H. había vivido en más de doce ciudades de su patria y del extranjero: Ciudad de México, Kansas, Buffalo, Colorado, Topeka, Cleveland, Chicago, etc. Recién graduado en segunda enseñanza desempeña diversos menesteres: mensajero, ayudante de un agricultor. Vuelta a México. Estudiante en la Universidad de Columbia. Se huye de la Universidad. Enrolado como marino, vivió como los hombres de río y de mar, sobre el Hudson, sobre el Atlántico, Islas Canarias, en la costa occidental del Africa. Nombres sugestivos cautivaron su oído y quedaron grabados para siempre en su espíritu: Dakar, Baratú, las Azores, la Afortunadas, la bahía de Loanda, Calabar, Lagos, el Congo Belga . . . Regresó a Nueva York y de nuevo el mar: Holanda, Paris, a donde llega con siete dólares en el bolsillo y en cuya ciudad su primer deseo realizado es contemplar largamente el Louvre y el teatro de la Opera—¡desde fuera!—para que si moría de hambre no se quedara sin cumplir ese anhelo de sus días infantiles. Portero en un cabaret de Montmartre. Segundo cocinero de un restaurant frecuentado por turistas. Viaje a Italia en idénticas condiciones que nuestro Pita Rodríguez—como amigo de toda una familia—¡en Italia, a pesar de Mussolini, no se han perdido aún todas las costumbres encantadoras! En Venecia le roban dinero y pasaporte. Vuelta a la miseria absoluta. En Génova: luchas obligadas con los "camisas negras." Vino, higos y macarrones. De nuevo a enrolarse como marino. Nápoles, de lejos. Sicilia, las islas de Lipari. Y España. La "divina España." Valencia. Y ya, Nueva York. El año 1924. En un baile público conoce la misma noche en que llega a su gran introductor ante el mundo: a Van Vechten. Más tarde la Universidad de Lincoln, donde se gradúa. Antes, la popularidad conveniente. Su historia llegó a los periódicos. En unión de sus poemas. Y comenzó su carrera de escritor. A todo lo largo de esa maravillosa *film*: Mujeres. Peleas. Contrabandistas. Marineros borrachos. Corrida de toros. "En cada puerto una novia," como en el poema de Alberti. Novias de todos colores. Negras. "Yeller." Rusas. Españolas. Mujeres y poemas.

Y en seguida, dinero por los poemas. Su nombre comenzó a aparecer y a prestigiar publicaciones como *Vanity Fair, Poetry, The New Republic, The New York Herald Tribune, The Modern Quarterly, The New Masses.* Y luego sus libros: *Weary Blues* (cinco ediciones en tres años), *Fine Clothes to the Jew* (dos ediciones en dos años). Y sus artículos a ser pagados en grande por periódicos y revistas "negros": *The Crisis, Opportunity.* Y ahora la novela: *Not Without Laughter* (Knopf, N. Y.) que aparecerá el próximo otoño.

Los versos de L. H. han sido traducidos ya al francés, al alemán y al ruso. En español y antes de los que aquí ofrecemos, sólo había sido traducido y publicado su famoso "I, too, sing America . . . " (*Social*, Septiembre de 1928) que reproducimos.

En la obra lírica de L. H.—como en toda la de Countee Cullen, Walter F. White, Jessie Fauscet, Claude MacKay, para no nombrar más que a los más representativos escritores de la raza negra en los Estados Unidos—está patente un vigoroso orgullo racial, una combatividad desconocida hasta el momento presente por parte de los productores intelectuales de esa raza. Su técnica es moderna y sus sensibilidad alcanza matices personalísimos que lo hacen destacar con propios lineamientos dentro del complicado panorama que es la contemporánea produción poética en los Estados Unidos.

L. H. durante su reciente visita a Cuba, fué recibido y festejado por los elementos representativos de nuestra joven intelectualidad, y por distinguidas personalidades y entidades cubanas de la raza negra. A su regreso a Nueva York, donde reside habitualmente, tiene el propósito de dar a conocer en inglés algunos poemas de escritores jóvenes de Cuba: Tallet, Guillén, Pedroso. También va a escribir sobre nuestros compositores actuales: Roldán, García Caturla.

Revista de la Habana, entre cuyos colaboradores cuenta L. H. entrañables amigos, se complace en ofrecer a sus lectores algunos de sus poemas en español, no sin advertirles que en la traducción han perdido a veces toda la fuerza e intensidad que poseen siempre en el original.

From: *Revista de la Habana* 1 (March 1930): 367-68.

Conversación con Langston Hughes

Nicolás Guillén

Los que no conocíamos a Langston Hughes más que de modo puramente intelectual, al través de "The Weary Blues" y de "Fine Clothes to the Jew," sus dos libros de versos, le atribuíamos una madurez física a la que no ha llegado todavía y la que tardará en llegar aún.

Por eso fue que cuando "el enfermo número 20," extraña denominación bajo la que ha estado viviendo durante varios días ese gran espíritu que es José Antonio Fernández de Castro, dio la voz de alarma y anunció la aparición del gran cantor negro, alguien me decía, mientras caminábamos sin orientación en busca del recién llegado: "Si yo veo a Mr. Hughes lo reconocería en seguida, porque conservo sus señas. Es un hombre du cuarenta o cuarenta y cinco años, alto, bastante grueso, casi blanco por el color de la piel, y con un bigotito inglés decorándole los labios finos y amargados."

Efectivamente: cuando apareció Mr. Hughes nos encontramos con un jovencito de veinte y siete años, menudo y delgado, de color trigueño, y que no usa bigote a la inglesa, ni a la moda de ninguna otra nación. Parece justamente un "mulatico" cubano. Uno de esos mulaticos intrascendentes, que estudian una carrera en la Univ. Nac. y que se pasan la vida organizando pequeñas fiestas familiares a dos pesos el billete. Sin embargo, detrás alienta uno de los espíritus más sinceramente interesados en las cosas de la raza negra, y un poeta personalísimo, sin más preocupación que la de observar su gente para traducirla, darla a conocer y hacerla amar. Él, antes que ningún otro poeta en su idioma, ha conseguido incorporar a la literatura norteamericana las manifestaciones más puras de la música popular en los E. U., tan influída por los negros. Sus "jazz poems," sus "blues poems" y sus "spirituals" son característicos.

Por lo demás, Mr. Hughes invita poco al reportaje profesional, porque es un hombre acogedor y amable, a quien uno prefiere irlo bailando lentamente, para verle salir de la bruma los contornos del espíritu, antes que explorarlo en una excursión circunstancial y cinematográfica.

Como pocos, el artista americano tiene la preocupación de los negros, de todo lo relacionado con los negros.

—"Ahora es una moda, ¿sabe usted?"—nos explica. "Pero a mí estas cosas me han interesado mucho siempre. Antes, en mí país, la moda era lo ruso. Hace seis años, el público no leía más que lit. de aquel pueblo. Era una fiebre. Hoy, nada interesa tanto como nosotros. Después, cuando nos toque pasar, yo creo que será lo indio. Lo indio de América, ¿sabe? Todo lo relativo a las razas autóctonas del Continente."

El castellano de Mr. Hughes no es muy rico. Pero él lo aprovecha maravillosamente. Siempre consigue decir lo que desea. Y, sobre todo, siempre tiene algo que decir.

Nos habla de su vida:

—"Yo debiera ser actualmente un profesional. Querían que me graduara abogado, o médico, o ingeniero. Pero, a la verdad, desde los catorce años yo no hacía más que poemas, mercancía que vale muy poco. Puedo decirle que esa es mi forma de reaccionar frente a la miseria de las clases humildes y frente a la terrible situación en que viven los negros en mi país. Después de haber estudiado un año en la Univ. de Columbia, me lancé a recorrer el mundo, libre de todas las trabas, al margen de todos los convencionalismos. Mi primer empleo fue en el campo, de labrador, ¿sabe Ud.?, y, más tarde, trabajé como camarero, en un barco, y como marinero también. Esta fue la época en que estuve en África.

—"¿En África?"

—"Sí, señor. He visitado Dakar, Nigeria, Loanda . . . Por aquellas tierras se me fortaleció el alma en el sentimiento de amor a los negros, que ya no habrá de abandonarme. En contacto con esa dulce gente, a la que Bélgica le corta los brazos y a la que Francia diezma brutalmente en la tala de bosques, como ha dado a conocer al mundo el periodista Alberto Londres, yo comprendí que era necesario ser su amigo, su voz, su báculo: ser su poeta. Yo no tengo más ambición que la de ser el poeta de los negros. El poeta negro, ¿comprende usted?"

Yo, sí comprendo. Y siento que se me sube del fondo del alma aquel poema con que este hombre abre su primer tomo de versos: "Yo, soy negro: negro, como la noche: negro como las profundidades de mi África."

—"Del África"—continúa Mr. Hughes—"pasé a Europa. Visité París, Milán, Venecia, Génova. Sufrí mucho. Trabajé en los oficios más humildes. Conocí de cerca los dolores del pueblo. Y regresé a mi patria sin un níquel, pagando con mis brazos el precio del pasaje. Desembarqué, pobre y roto, una tarde de invierno en N. Y. Por la noche estuve en Harlem. Mis versos tuvieron la suerte de interesar. Me ayudaron algunos amigos. Y en 1926 publiqué mi primer libro, *The Weary Blues,* en el que figuran mis poemas negros, mis poemas de jazz, escritos para esta clase de música: mis poemas de mar, de cuando yo andaba descalzo sobre la cubierta de los barcos, en África y en Europa: y mis poemas de amor, que también hubo tiempo para amar . . .

—"¿Y después?:

—"Después apareció mi segundo tomo de versos, *Fine Clothes to the Jew.* Contiene *blues* y *spirituals,* manifestaciones ambos de la música popular negra americana, y, además, varios poemas raciales y de trabajo. Siempre con mi pueblo, ¿sabe usted? Ahora, en agosto, saldrá mi última obra. Una novela titulada *Not Without Laughter,* en la que describo la vida de una familia negra de la parte central de los E. U., y en la que trato de enseñar como a pesar de los grandes dolores del negro americano y de su formidable lucha contra el prejuicio blanco, la nota risueña esmalta a menudo su tragedia. Ya están los originales en poder del editor."

—"¿Cómo ve usted"—le pregunto—"el problema de razas en los E. U., en lo que toca a la negra? ¿Se adelanta en la solución? Me gustaría conocer lo que usted opina . . . "

El poeta sonríe. Juega con la sortija de su Univ., donde relampaguea, en oro, el sello tradicional y al fin nos responde:

—"Mire usted, yo no soy un sociólogo científico. No he hecho estudios para ello. Soy simplemente un poeta. Vivo entre los míos; los amo; me duelen en la entraña los golpes que reciben y canto sus dolores, traduzco sus tristezas, echo a volar sus ansias. Y eso lo hago a la manera del pueblo, con la misma sencillez con que el pueblo lo hace. ¿Usted no sabe que jamás me he preocupado de estudiar las reglas clásicas del verso? Yo tengo la suerte de no haber escrito nunca un soneto, ¿sabe usted? Escribo lo que me viene desde adentro. Igual lo podría cantar, como hacían los antiguos. Yo no "estudio" al negro. Lo "siento."

Después, completando su idea, nos dice:

—"Yo sólo aspiro a conservarle al negro su frescura, a que no olvide nunca lo que es suyo. Me parece que la civilización blanca puede acabar lo primitivo que hay en el negro, vistiéndolo con un ropaje que no será de él jamás. Por supuesto, que hay muchos negros que me combaten porque estiman que algunos de mis poemas sólo están dedicados a la gente baja, al subsuelo, y ellos se entretienen jugando a la aristocracia, a la "high life," para imitar a sus antiguos amos! . . . Pero, ¡qué va uno a hacer! . . .

El negro Cuba es, en sus elementos más íntimos, la constante preocupación de Mr. H. Por donde quiera que pasa, indaga por el negro.

"¿Vienen negros a este café?"—pregunta. ¿En esta orquesta no admiten negros? ¿No hay artistas negros aquí? ¡Me gustaría ir a un cabaret de negros en la Habana! . . .

Lo llevo a una academia de baile, de esas en que sólo danzan los individuos de nuestra raza. Desde que penetra en el local, el poeta está como poseído del espíritu de los *suezos*—de lo mío.

—"¡Mi gente!"—exclama.

Y se queda largamente junto a la orquesta escandalosa en que un "son" esparce su humo verde, para seguir, con la respiración entrecortada por la emoción, el ritmo, nuevo en su espíritu. Después, mientras contempla al bongosero, "negro como la noche," exclama, con un suspiro de ansia insatisfecha:

—"Yo quisiera ser negro. Bien negro. ¡Negro de verdad!"

Diario de la Marina 98, no. 68 (9 March 1930) p. 6.

Notas sobre la Poesía de los Negros
en los Estados Unidos

Salvador Novo

Un país tan cosmopolita como los Estados Unidos ofrece, como ningún otro, campo propicio al regionalismo. El organillo italiano, el pequeño usurero judío y Carmen cupletista, constituyen otros tantos pequeños mundos cuya supervivencia ha dependido en mucho de su personal acomodación a la imagen que de ellos se ha querido formar el norteamericano. El caso de los poetas negros, como el de los negros en general, en los Estados Unidos, se agrava por el hecho de que existe, como es visible, una especie de represión en los norteamericanos, en cuyo teatral siglo XIX juegan los negros un papel de troyanos que proporcionan, entre los campos de algodón, el necesario contraste en que se mueve la prosaica epopeya de la novela de Harriet Beecher Stowe. Con su lectura, los negros adquirieron un sentido de lastimera importancia al que iba unido el secreto de una actitud de víctimas que habría de garantizar su éxito. Y es curioso observar la transferencia de una actitud que es un "mea culpa" en el caso de los compasivos escritores norteamericanos, a los negros mismos, cuya lira monocorde hará vibrar su acento de un siglo al otro.

Pocas antologías poéticas se atreverían a incluir en sus páginas producciones de poetas negros. Y cuando lo hagan, como lo hace Louis Untermeyer, escogerán poesías en dialecto de Paul Laurence Dunbar (1872–1906), patriarca de los poetas negros de América, cuya mayor preocupación era precisamente la de no concentrarse en el dialecto.

Asunto frecuente de dramas modernos desde "All God's Chillun got Wings" de O'Neill, hasta "Green Pastures", el negro intelectual norteamericano ha vivido en el dilema de olvidar su color y de superarlo haciéndolo olvidar, para sumarse al general parnaso—y en este caso se aplica a las más puras normas de versificación inglesa y habla en difícil—o de aceptar su sitio social, con todas las implicaciones de humillación injusta y de insinuación de valores profundos, de aptitudes estéticas que con su fuerza equilibrarían, en un mundo menos imperfecto, una simple "anomalía pigmentaria."

En tanto, su música muscular, sensual, útil como un aullido, se apoderó de los Estados Unidos. Los *blues,* que atacan por igual al portero del pullman que al millonario que viaja en él, y el lap, llegaron a unir, por diferentes rutas, al blanco y al negro cuando ambos expresan, bailándolo, la alegría de reproducir los impulsos ancestrales que todos llevamos en el subconsciente colectivo de Jung. Los *blues* abren a los poetas negros de los Estados Unidos una puerta más hacia el éxito. Los cultiva con preferente delectación. Y luego existe un Sherwood Anderson que los da ejemplo de refinado primitivismo, y un Vachel Lindsay que haya cantado con sus ritmos genuinos, y hay para las mujeres una Sara Teasdale que imitar. Poco a poco, los poetas negros—como los judíos, como los italianos—irán abandonando el dialecto. El reconocimiento universal de su calidad de poetas (los versos suyos empiezan a aparecer en revistas y en antologías europeas) los animará a continuar una obra que ofrece ya características de singular valor, pero cuya aspiración parece todavía la de incorporarse a la poesía norteamericana cuyos colores borra su generalidad.

El primer negro de quien se sabe que haya escrito poesía en los Estados Unidos es Phyllis Wheatley. El primero que logró la incorporación a la poesía norteamericana fue Paul Laurence Dunbar. De este alto poeta en adelante, hay no menos de veinte poetas negros, de buena calidad algunos, como Richard Bruce, Waring Cunney y Edward S. Silvera, nacidos en 1906. Countee Cullen, autor de tres libros de versos y de una Antología de la Poesía Negra, y Langston Hughes, de quien han aparecido traduciones en "Sur" recientemente, nacieron, respectivamente, en 1903 y 1902. Langston Hughes es seguramente uno de los más interesantes poetas negros del momento. Vagabundo, estuvo en México durante quince meses, aprendió español, enseñó inglés, fue a las corridas de toros y escribió su primer poema publicado en revistas: "El Negro habla de los Ríos."

De aquí fue a Nueva York y viajó luego al África y a Europa como marino en barcos de carga. Ha sido portero en un Cabaret de

Montmartre y cocinero en un Cabaret Negro. Vachel Lindsay lo
descubrió—.

From: *Contemporáneos* 11 (September-October 1931): 197–200.

Langston Hughes, El Poeta Afro-
Estadounidense

Rafael Lozano

Difícilmente existe un individuo que a los veintiocho años de edad, haya gozado de una existencia tan pintoresca y tan azarosa como Langston Hughes, el más joven y el más interesante de los poetas negros de los Estados Unidos. Un relato completo de su vida, desordenada y deliciosamente fantástica, podría formar una auténtica novela picaresca. Y es de desearse que este joven negro se decida a escribirla antes de que el cúmulo de sus aventuras le hagan casi imposible encerrar, en las páginas de un solo volumen, los sucesos más importantes en que ha actuado como protagonista.

Nuestro poeta nació el primero de febrero de mil novecientos dos, en la población de Joplin, perteneciente al Estado de Missouri. Antes de cumplir los doce años ya había vivido en juestra capital; en Topeka, Kansas; en Colorado Springs; en Charlestown, Indiana; en Kansas City, y en Buffalo. Hizo sus estudios preparatorios en la Central High School de Cleveland, Ohio, donde, en el año de su gradución, fue elegido, de acuerdo con una típica costumbre estudiantil de los Estados Unidos, poeta de su clase y director del anuario escolar.

Permaneció cuatro años más en Cleveland, al cabo de los cuales vino otra vez a la ciudad de México para visitar a su padre, regresando inmediatamente a nueva York, donde ingresó a la Universidad de Columbia, cuyo ambiente estudiantil y escolástico le fue tan desagradable que, a los pocos meses, abandonó sus estudios, lo que fue causa de una ruptura definitiva con su padre; y, con trece dólares en el bolsillo, se lanzó a la aventura. Primero, trabajó como chofer de un camión de carga en un rancho de Staten Island; después, entró como repartidor de una famosa casa de flores en Nueva York; al fin, satisfizo en parte sus irrefrenables deseos de hacer vida de mar enganchándose en un viejo barco que estaba anclado durante el invierno en el río Hudson.

Su primera travesía como marinero lo llevó a las Islas Canarias, a Los Azores y a la costa oeste de Africa. Langston Hughes ha escrito, al recordar ese viaje: "¡Oh, el sol de Dakar! ¡Oh, las negritas de Burutu! ¡Oh, la bahía azul, tan azul, de Loanda! ¡Oh, Calabar, la ciudad perdida en el bosque; los largos y esplendorosos días en altamar; los mástiles meciéndose en la noche, bajo las estrellas; los marineros negros de Kru, enganchados en Freetown, y bañándose sobre cubierta en la mañana y en la noche; los dos muchachos, Tom Pey y Hanco, cuya peligrosa misión era la de nadar bajo los troncos de caoba de siete toneladas, que flotaban meciéndose cerca del barco, y amarrarlos a las cadenas de las grúas; los redrojos de las casas viles de Lagos; la desolación del Congo; Johnny Walker y los millones de botellas de whisky sepultadas en el mar a lo largo de la costa oeste de Africa; las riñas diarias a bordo, de los oficiales, de los marineros y de toda la tripulación ebria; los timoratos y asustadizos misioneros que llevábamos como pasaje; George, el muchacho negro de Kentucky, cantando y bailando blues en la segunda cubierta y bajo las estrellas."

Regresó a Nueva York, con bastante dinero y un mono, para embarcarse de nuevo e inmediatamente, esta vez con rumbo a Holanda. Regresó una segunda vez a Nueva York y se volvió a embarcar, en su vigésimo segundo aniversario, el primero de febrero de mil novecientos veinticuatro. Tres semanas después, se encontraba en París con menos de siete dólares en el bolsillo. Sin embargo, pronto tuvo quien lo ayudara, pues una mujer de su propia raza le dió empleo como portero de su boite de nuit. Después encontró trabajo como segundo cocinero y, un poco después, como mesero en el cabaret Gran Duc, donde a la sazón cantaba la célebre Florence Mills. Ahí trabó amistad con una rica familia italiana que se lo llevó a su villa en Desenzano, en el Lago di Garda, donde pasó un mes absolutamente dichoso, seguido de una noche en Verona y de una semana en Venecia.

Durante su viaje de regreso, a través de Italia, le robaron su pasaporte y se hizo estibador en los muelles de Génova. Con su estilo pintoresco, nos escribe su vida en aquella época. "Vino, higos y pasta. Y sol, ¡mucho sol!" Y por compañeros bizarros, todos los otros estibadores que vagabundeaban por los muelles y por las calles del puerto, provocando a los fascistas con sus constantes grescas y partiendo una pieza de pan en tantos pedazos que nadie alcanzaba más que migajas. Viví en los jardines públicos, cerca de los muelles, y dormí en el Albergo Populare a razón de dos liras por noche, y entre los ronquidos de otros cientos de golfos. . . . Me gané mi regreso pintando el barco en que venía. Ahora me parece que debí de haber pintado todo el buque. Hicimos lo que se llama una travesía de lujo: Livorno y Nápoles, pasando tan cerca de Capri que sentí ganas de llorar; después, al derredor de Sicilia Catania, Mesina y Palermo; las islas Lipari, insignificantes montículos de piedra pómez asomando sus crestas sobre el mar; luego, la costa de España, ¡la divina España! Mi cuate y yo fuimos a echar una cana al aire en Valencia, durante una noche y un día. ¡Oh el dulce vino de Valencia!" Por fin, Nueva York, a donde llegó el diez de noviembre de mil novecientos veinticuatro.

Esa noche lo conoció en una fiesta dada por la Asociación Nacional para el Progreso de la Gente de Color, Carl Van Vechten, autor de una admirable novela sobre el ambiente de Harlem, el barrio negro de Nueva York, intitulada *Paraíso Negro,* y a quien debo una buena parte de los datos que dejo pergeñados. "Ojalá que este joven negro," dice Carl Van Vechten hablando de Langston Hughes, "se decida a confiar al papel, en sus más nimios detalles, las corridas de toros en México; la ebria alegría del Grand Duc; la delicada y exquisita gracia de las negritas de Burutu; la exótica languidez de las mujeres españolas de Valencia; los bailes bárbaros al son del jazz, en Harlem, en el corazón de Nueva York; la camaradería de los marineros de diversas razas y nacionalidades; todo, en una palabra, lo que ha dejado una marca indeleble en la sensibilidad hiperestesiada de este joven negro y que ya ha encontrado su expresión inicial en los versos que ha escrito y que ha reunido en un volumen que ha titulado, *The Weary Blues.*"

La poesía de Langston Hughes es eminentemente espontánea. Tiene esa natural negligencia, nacida de la emoción de que nos habla Charles Guerin. Lo mismo canta a las prostitutas negras de Harlem, que a una placera de México, o a sus compañeros de mar. Pero en todos sus versos se advierte la nota personal, la observación directa, desliteraturizada, vivida intensamente y sentida hasta el paroxismo. No es suprarealista, ni mallarmeano, ni siquiera ha sufrido la influencia de Baudelaire, del Baudelaire de *Albatros* y del amor por lo exótico. Es un cantor primitivo, como todos los de su raza, que se expresa en ritmos propios, un poco sincopados, como la música del jazz.

From: *Crisol: Revista de crítica* 5 (March 1931): 225–27.

Bibliography

Alberto, Santos. "El poeta Langston Hughes nos visita de nuevo." *Diario de la Marina* 8 April 1931, p. 2.

Augier, Angel. *Nicolás Guillén: Notas para un estudio biográfico-crítico.* 2 vols. Santa Clara, Cuba: Universidad Central de las Villas, 1965.

———. "La raíz cubana." *Recopilación de textos sobre Nicolás Guillén.* Havana: Casa de las Américas, 1974, pp. 139–46.

Ayala, Leopoldo. "Réquiem para la tumba de un cuerpo." *Poesía joven de México.* Mexico: Siglo Veinte, 1968, pp. 40–42.

Ballagas, Emilio. *Antología de la poesía negra americana.* Buenos Aires: Pleamar, 1946.

———. *Antología de la poesía negra-hispanoamericana.* Madrid: Aguilar, 1935.

Bohórquez, Abigael. "Carta abierta a Langston Hughes." *La Palabra y el Hombre* 6 (January-March 1962): 147–52.

Boti, Regino E. "La poesía cubana de Nicolás Guillén." *Revista Bimestre Cubana* 29 (May-June 1932): 343–53.

Cardoza y Aragón, Luis. "Langston Hughes, el poeta de los negros." *El Nacional* 17 March 1935, p. 6.

Coulthard, G. R. *Race and Colour in Caribbean Literature.* London: Oxford Press, 1962. Basic study of Caribbean literature.

Cunard, Nancy. "Three Negro Poets." *Left Review* 2 (October 1937): 529–36.

Dodat, François. *Langston Hughes.* Paris: Seghers, 1964.

Fernández de Castro, José Antonio. "Langston Hughes, poeta militante negro." *El Nacional* 3 March 1935, p. 1.

———. "Presentación de Langston Hughes." *Revista de la Habana* 1, 3 (March 1930): 367–68.

Fernández de la Vega, Oscar, et al. *Iniciación a la poesía afroamericana.* Miami: Ediciones Universal, 1973.

Ferrer, José. "Langston Hughes: El cantor de las penas de la raza de color ha tenido contacto con la cultura hispánica." *Repertorio Americano* 49 (1955): 104–106.

Figueira, Gastón. "Dos poetas norteamericanos: I. Sinclair Lewis; II. Langston Hughes." *Revista Iberoamericana* 18 (January-September 1953): 401–404.

———. "Langston Hughes, voz de una raza." *Sustancia: Revista de Cultura Superior* 12 (July 1942): 260–65.

Florit, Eugenio. *Antología de la poesía norteamericana contemporánea,* Washington: Unión Panamericana, 1955.

González, José Luis. "La muerte de dos grandes escritores norteamericanos." *Siempre: Presencia de México* 729 (14 June 1967): v–ix.

González Flores, Manuel. *Una pareja de tantas,* México: Editorial Yolotepec, 1950.

"El gran poeta negro norteamericano Langston Hughes." *Nivel* 31 (25 July 1961): xv.

"El gran poeta negro Langston Hughes regresa a los EE.UU." *Nivel* 46 (25 October 1962): 6.

Guillén, Nicolás. "Conversación con Langston Hughes. "*Diario de la Marina* 9 March 1930, p. 6.

———. "A Conversation with Langston Hughes." Trans. E. J. Mullen. *Caliban: A Journal of New World Writing.* 2 (Fall-Winter 1976), 123–26.

———. "Le souvenir de Langston Hughes," *Présence Africaine* 64 (October-December 1967): 34–37.

Guirao, Ramón, ed. *Órbita de la poesía afro-cubana, 1928–37.* Havana: Ugar, García y Cía, 1938.

Gunn, Dewey W. *American and British Writers in Mexico, 1556–1973.* Austin: University of Texas Press, 1974, pp. 80–86.

Henestrosa, Andrés. "Un Extraño Suceso." *Novedades* 8 June 1967, p. 4, cols. 3–4.

———. "Un poeta negro." *Novedades* 1 June 1967, p. 4, cols. 3–4.

Hernández Urbina, Francisco. "Vida y muerte del poeta Langston Hughes," *Universidad Central* 13 April 1961, pp. 16–17.

Jackson, Richard L. "Black Phobia and the White Aesthetic in Spanish American Literature." *Hispania* 58 (1975): 467–80.

Johnson, Lemuel A. *The Devil, The Gargoyle, and the Buffoon: The Negro as Metaphor in Western World Literature.* Port Washington, N.Y.: Kennikat Press, 1971.

Lozano, Rafael. "Langston Hughes, el poeta afroestadounidense." *Crisol: Revista de Crítica* 5 (March 1931): 225–27.

Mansour, Mónica. *La poesía negrista.* México: Ediciones Era, 1973, p. 137.

Marco, Pedro. "Canción de la calle." *Diario de la Marina* 16 March 1930, p. 6.

Matheus, John F. "Langston Hughes as Translator." *Langston Hughes Black Genius,* ed. Therman B. O'Daniel. New York: William Morrow, 1971, pp. 157–70.

McMurray, David Arthur. "Dos negros en el Nuevo Mundo: Notas sobre el 'americanismo' del Langston Hughes y la Cubanía de Nicolás Guillén." *Casa de las Américas* 14 (January-February 1974): 122–28.

Mejía Sánchez, Ernesto. Review of *Yo también soy América. Amaru, Revista de Artes y Ciencias* (April-June 1968): 95.

Mueller-Berg, Klaus. *Alejo Carpentier: Estudio biográfico-crítico.* New York: Las Américas, 1972, pp. 27–28.

Mullen, E. J. "European and North American Writers in *Contemporáneos.*" *Comparative Literature Studies* 8 (December 1971): 338–46.

———. "Langston Hughes y la crítica literaria hispanoamerica." *Memoria del XV Congreso del Instituto Internacional de Literatura Iberoamericana.* Madrid: Cultura Hispánica (in press). A study of Hughes and Spanish-American critics.

———. "Langston Hughes y Nicolás Guillén: Un documento y un comentario." *Caribe* (in press). Reproduces interview with Guillen.

———. "Presencia y evaluación de Langston Hughes en Hispanoamérica." *Revista de la Comunidad Latinoamericana de Escritores* 15 (1974): 16–21.

Noble, Enrique. "Aspectos étnicos y sociales de la poesía mulata latinoamericana." *Revista Bimestre Cubana* 40 (January-June 1958): 166–79.

_____. "Nicolás Guillén y Langston Hughes." *Nueva Revista Cubana*. Havana: Editora del Consejo Nacional de Cultura, 1962, pp. 3–47.

Novás Calvo, Lino. "El que cantó Harlem, Canta China y España." *Ayuda* 18 September 1937, p. 3.

Novo, Salvador. "Notas sobre la poesía de los negros en los Estados Unidos." *Contemporáneos* 11 (September-October 1931): 197–200.

_____. "Notes on Black Poetry in the United States." trans. E. J. Mullen. *Review 76* no. 17 (Spring 1976): 21–22.

Ortiz Avila, Raúl. "El Ruiseñor y la Prosa." *El Nacional* 20 April 1952, p. 12.

_____. Ibid., *El Nacional* 27 April 1952, p. 12.

Ortiz, Fernando de. "Motivos de son, por Nicolás Guillén." *Archivos del Folklore Cubano* 5 (July-September 1930): 222–38.

Portuondo, José Antonio. *Bosquejo histórico de las letras cubanas.* Havana: Editora del Ministerio de Educación, 1962.

Tejera, Humberto. "Langston Hughes en México." *El Nacional* 28 November 1948, pp. 5 and 28.

Urrutia, Gustavo. "El Paraíso de los negros." *Diario de la Marina* 27 September 1932, p. 2.

Vitier, Cintio. *Lo cubano en la poesía.* Havana: Ucar García y Cia, 1958.

Wagner, Jean. "El gran poeta negro norteamericano Langston Hughes." *Nivel* 31 (25 July 1961): 5.

Zardoya, Concha. "Dos poemas de Langston Hughes." *Insula* 248–49 (1967): 24.

Index